#1

Author:

EMMI SALONEN

COMMON INTEREST: DOCUMENTS

Design and format solutions for the arts, culture, academia and charities

COMMON INTEREST: DOCUMENTS

Published by:
Index Book, S.L.
Consell de Cent 160 local 3
08015 Barcelona
Spain
T: +34 934 545 547
F: +34 934 548 438
ib@indexbook.com
www.indexbook.com

Publisher:
Sylvie Estrada

Author and Art Director:
Emmi Salonen

Design:
Studio EMMI
www.emmi.co.uk

ISBN: 978-84-92643-53-0

Author:

EMMI SALONEN

COMMON INTEREST: DOCUMENTS

Design and format solutions for the arts, culture, academia and charities

Contents:

Introduction:

DESIGN AND THE COMMON GOOD

This book showcases document designs, including leaflets, brochures and books, designed for organisations that exist to provide a positive experience through learning, creating an event or providing a structure for the individual to better themselves. The chapters are organised by sector; academia, art, charity and culture, highlighting how even within the showcased fields the works are very varied. For many of these documents environmental considerations are an integral part of the design and the production process.

The common element of the sectors featured here is the need to appeal to a wide and varied public, so the designs must be attractive across the board. Eliminating exclusivity makes them 'open for all' and the experience becomes a shared one. The documents are also often made to be physically accessible by all, due to their distribution throughout public spaces, cultural events and galleries.

From a designer's point of view, laying out a book or brochure requires thinking in sequences – something that only serves to make these documents more compelling. Printed work often has a short life, existing only for the duration of the event or an exhibition. If the document is beautifully crafted, however, it can become collectable and

people want to hold on to them as ephemera or inspiration. Some books may even become heirlooms - kept and passed down through generations.

In most cases designers aren't only concerned about the visuals but are also required to operate within a limited budget. Budget considerations can become part of the design solution as illustrated later on in the book.

In addition, this book attempts to provide guidance for designers through the working process, showing common paper sizes, formats and information on preparing work for print. These are meant as suggestions only and each designer should add and alter them as they see fit. *Common Interest* aims to inspire new thinking throughout the creative process and to open the way for unique and groundbreaking ideas and designs for the future.

Environment:

COMMON INTEREST: ENVIRONMENT

As designers and commissioners of design, we can make environmental considerations a vital part of the design process. It is not always possible to make each design 100 per cent environmentally sound, but we can aim to do our best. This book showcases many design solutions that have reduced their environmental impact beyond the given brief. At the back of the book, there is also a list of environmental considerations to keep in mind throughout the design process. p. 185

Often the first thing that comes to mind when thinking about sustainable design is recycled paper. Specifying environmentally friendly paper is certainly a good start. There are multiple paper options to choose from, ranging from recycled paper with various percentages of recycled fibre, to those where the energy came from to create the paper has been considered (some use wind power), as well as the amount of water and emissions involved in the process. A recycled paper that is certified by the Forest Stewardship Council (FSC) is always a good environmental choice.

Choice is the key word in the environmental discussion, whether that relates to specifying items for print or to the general running of a studio. Some green options are more environmentally friendly than others.

Before making any selections it is important to look at all the available options. Some companies choose to reduce their carbon footprint, some limit their use of resources and others are focused towards providing more sustainably sourced alternatives. It is not always possible to cover all the areas and use a product or service that meets the top marks on all, so the best advice is to research carefully and decide what matters the most to you when selecting material, choosing a printer and setting up your studio space.

Common Interest includes case studies that are examples of efficient print solutions and production processes, such as using vegetable-based inks or incorporating attractive alternatives to finishings like foil blocking (which may make the final item unrecyclable due to not breaking down during the de-inking process). In some cases literature is designed in a way that it can be updated easily, reducing the need to printing new copies whenever changes are required, thus reducing costs and use of resources.

This book serves as a brief introduction to the subject with the hope that it might inspire designers to consider more environmentally friendly design solutions and practices, while encouraging those studios that already do to carry on.

Format:

COMMON PAPER SIZES

There are real benefits for checking the sheet size of the paper you have chosen to use, and finding out from your printer what press size they are using. Maximising the use of paper can have a real effect on reducing waste in the production and could mean extra copies for the same cost.

Papers come in many size categories but the most common one is the ISO paper system, as seen on the right. ISO paper sizes are derived from an A0 size rectangle, which has the area of one square meter. In other words, the width and the height of a page relate to each other like the side and the diagonal of a square. There are a number of different paper 'series' that use the ISO system for determining sizes:

1. A-sizes are used to define the finished paper size
2. B-sizes allow for oversized formats and are often used for posters for example
3. C-sizes are used for envelopes to match the A-series paper
4. RA-sizes are used by printers to allow grip on the printing press
5. SRA-sizes are used by printers to allow for both grip and bleed

A0

A1

A3

A2

A5

A4

A6

A SERIES (mm)

A0	841 x 1189
A1	594 x 841
A2	420 x 594
A3	297 x 420
A4	210 x 297
A5	148 x 210
A6	105 x 148

B SERIES (mm)

B0	1000 x 1414
B1	707 x 1000
B2	500 x 707
B3	353 x 500
B4	250 x 353
B5	176 x 250
B6	125 x 176

C SERIES (mm)

C2	458 x 648
C3	324 x 458
C4	229 x 324
C5	162 x 229
C6	114 x 162

RA SERIES (mm)

RA0	860 x 11220
RA1	610 x 860
RA2	430 x 610
RA3	305 x 430
RA4	215 x 305

SRA SERIES (mm)

SRA0	900 x 1280
SRA1	640 x 900
SRA2	450 x 640
SRA3	320 x 450
SRA4	125 x 320

STANDARD US (″/mm)

8.5″ x 11″	216 x 280
17.5″ x 22.5″	445 x 572
19″ x 25″	483 x 635
23″ x 29″	584 x 737
23″ x 35″	584 x 889
24″ x 36″	610 x 914
25″ x 38″	635 x 965
35″ x 45″	889 x 1143

Format:

COMMON FOLDS

Imaginative use of folds can bring a piece of print to life and could be used as an alternative design element to avoid less environmentally friendly solutions like non-recyclable foils or lamination.

There are some considerations to bear in mind when folding paper or board. It is advisable to fold the paper parallel with the grain of the paper, as this will fold more cleanly and easily. This also means that the paper is less likely to break or look ragged. It makes the turning of pages more smooth and natural in feel.

A paper's grain is the direction in which most of the fibres lie. Paper can be either short or long grain, depending on how it is cut.

Paying attention to these details means you maximise both your paper and printing investments by avoiding costly reprints.

LONG GRAIN
The fibres run parallel to the paper's long side.

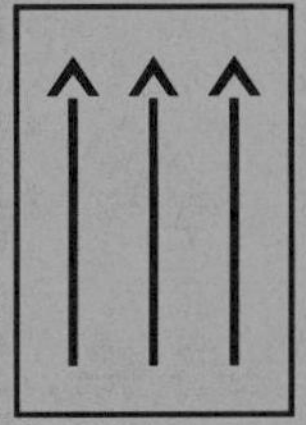

SHORT GRAIN
The fibres run parallel to the paper's short side.

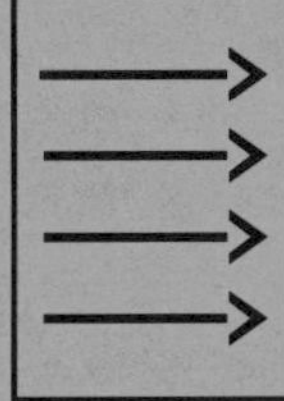

Format:

SINGLE FOLD

Format:

SHORT FOLD

Format:

LETTER FOLD / C-FOLD

Format:

6-PAGE ACCORDION / Z-FOLD

Format:

8-PAGE ACCORDION

Format:

DOUBLE FOLD / DOUBLE PARALLEL FOLD

Format:

BARREL / ROLL FOLD

Format:

MAP FOLD

Format:

RIGHT ANGLE WITH SHORT FOLD

Format:

GATE FOLD

Format:

RIGHT ANGLE / FRENCH FOLD

Format:

16-PAGE PARALLEL BOOKLET

Chapter One:

ACADEMIA

Academia:

The case studies featured in this chapter are either created by a commissioned designer or designed in-house. In the latter examples, the team includes a group of students who worked on a project together with a tutor.

One example of collective work is 'Dear Lulu' by University of Applied Sciences of Darmstadt, Germany. Run by Professor Frank Philippin and designer James Goggin, 'Dear Lulu' is a testbook which was researched and produced by graphic design students during an intensive two-day workshop. The book's intention is to act as a calibration document for testing colour, pattern, format, texture and typography. Exercises in halftoning, point size, line, skin tone and cropping provide useful data for other designers and self-publishers to judge the possibilities and quality of online print on demand, specifically Lulu.com with this edition. p. 42

Print on demand is a good resource-saving alternative to printing in volumes, making it a desirable environmentally friendly method. Any book produced can also be offered for sale which makes it an ideal solution for individuals to make fanzines or books, for example.

This chapter features varied examples of how designers have created works for the academic sector, including many that are successful far beyond the initial requirements of the brief.

Design

Client

UNFOLDED

ZHDK, SWITZERLAND

Title

Theaterpädagogik

Specifications

Size:
105mm x 148mm, folded
210mm x 297mm, flat

Colour & Print:
1-colour, offset

Folding:
A4 folded twice to A6

Design | **Client**

THE LUXURY OF PROTEST | **ROYAL COLLEGE OF ART, UK**

Title
Research RCA Exhibition Catalogue

Specifications
Size:
105mm x 148mm, folded
313mm x 444mm, flat
Colour & Print:
1-colour (PMS Black), offset
Paper:
Arjo Wiggins Curious Metallics,
White Gold, 120gsm
Folding:
the piece folds down and tucks
into an A5 pamphlet
Finishing:
yellow-gold foil stamp

Information graphics by
Karin von Ompteda

Finishing:

RCA WORK
27 NO
4 DE
'09
SELEC
-ION.
RESEARC

Design

LA FABRICA DE DISEÑO

Client

FAC. INFORMATION SCIENCES, UCM, SPAIN

Title

Torán

Specifications

Size:
210mm x 240mm, 156 pages with 8-page cover

Colour & Print:
2-colour, offset

Paper:
FEELme texturado, 300gsm

Binding:
section sewn

Finishing:
UV varnish

Format:

8-PAGE COVER

Design	Client
UNFOLDED	ZHDK, SWITZERLAND

Title
Bachelor of Arts

Specifications
Size:
148mm x 210mm, folded
420mm x 594mm, flat
Colour & Print:
1-colour and CMYK, offset
Paper:
Lesebo Ivory 1.3, 80gsm

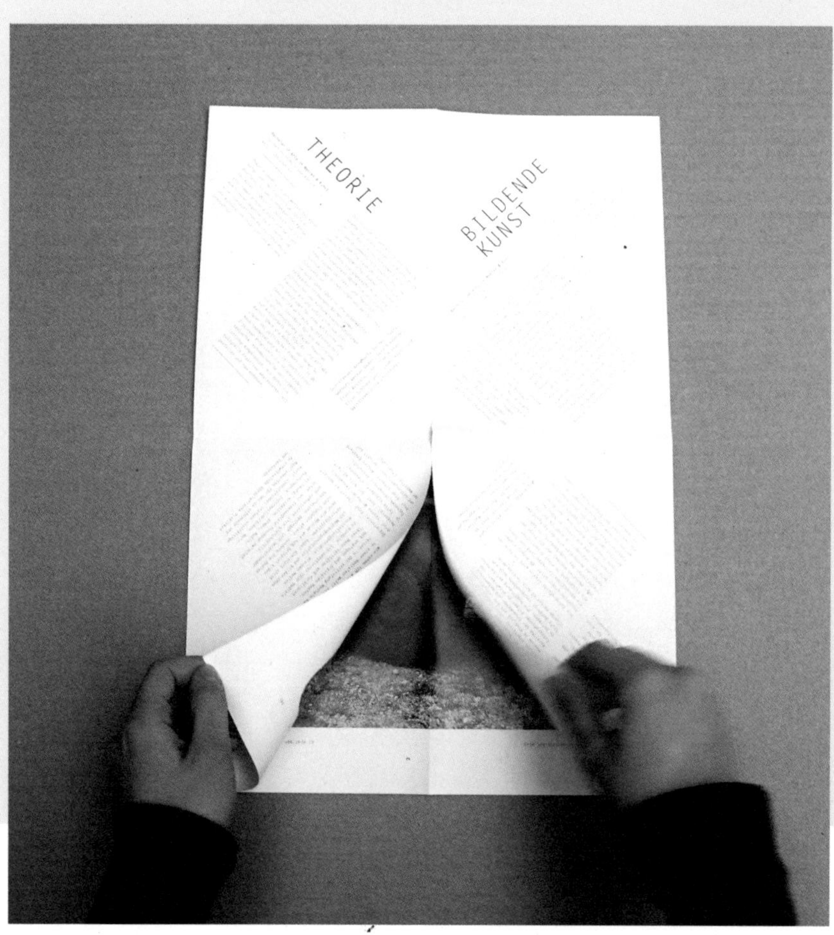

THEORIE
BILDENDE
KUNST
MEDIALE
KÜNSTE
FOTOGRAFIE
THEORIE

Design

BRUKETA&ZINIC OM

Client

5. GIMNAZIJA ZAGREB, CROATIA

Title
5th Gimnazija Monograph

Specifications
Colour & Print:
2-colour, offset
Paper:
cover: Munken Polar, 300gsm
inner pages: Munken Polar, 120gsm
Binding:
perfect bind

This school monograph was designed in the format of a functional pencil case.

PREDMET
IME I PREZIME
gimnazija

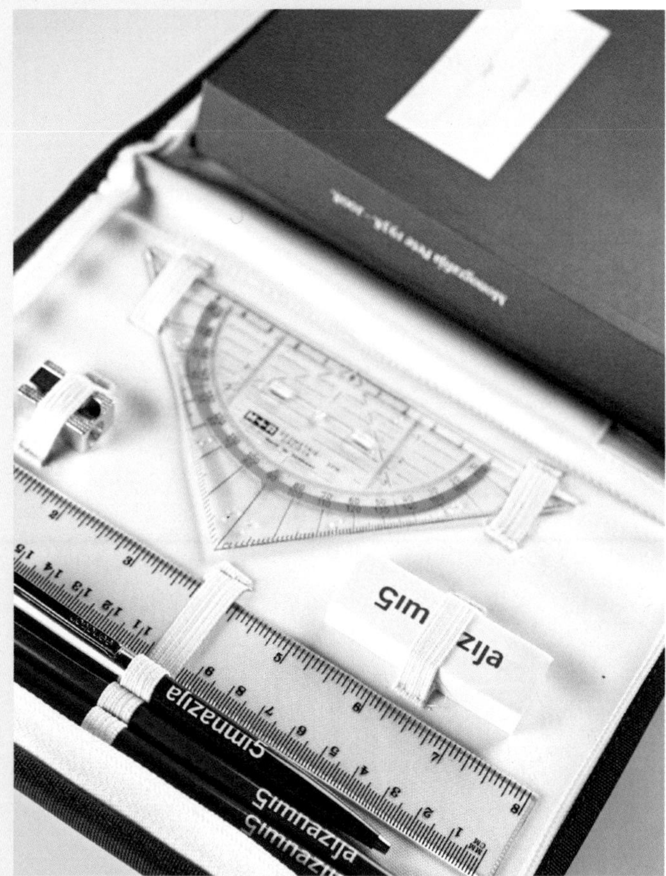
gimnazija

Design

STUDIO EMMI

Client

UNIVERSITY OF WESTMINSTER, UK

Title

Degree Show Catalogue

Specifications

Size:

A5, 36 pages plus 8-page cover

Colour & Print:

cover: CMYK

inner pages: 1-colour (black)

Folding:

covers are folded in, creating an 8-page cover

Binding:

saddle stitch

TITLE
MENTS

PAGE
TITLE

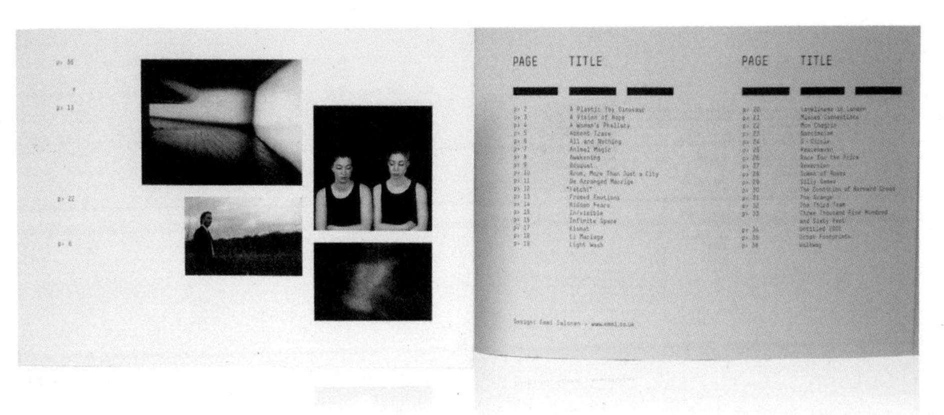
PAGE
TITLE
PAGE
TITLE

Design

BERMER&CO.

Client

CAJA NAVARRA, SPAIN

Title

Seminar at yhe Wharton School,
University of Pennsylvania

Specifications

Size:
90mm x 215mm, folded
540mm x 430mm, flat

Colour & Print:
CMYK

Paper:
Torraspapel, sepia, 80gsm

Folding:
6-page accordion

Folding:

6-PAGE ACCORDION

Design | **Client**

CONNIE HWANG DESIGN | **UNIVERSITY GALLERIES, USA**

Title
Ten Plus Ten: Revisiting Patterns and Decoration Exhibition catalogue

Specifications

Size:
A6, 16 pages plus cover wrap

Colour & Print:
catalogue: CMYK
wrap: 1-colour (Pantone metallic)

Folding:
accordion fold

Finishing:
deboss and diecut

Design	Client
HOCHSCHULE DARMSTADT	FACULTY OF DESIGN, GERMANY

Title
Summer Diplomas 08

Specifications
Size:
A1 poster, folded to A3
A7 book, 140 pages
A6 postcards
Colour & Print:
2-colour, offset
black and gold silkscreen
Finishing:
hand drawings and writings

The poster was printed with an empty bubble, which worked as a base for freely hand-drawn sketches. An announcement was then printed on top of the two layers.

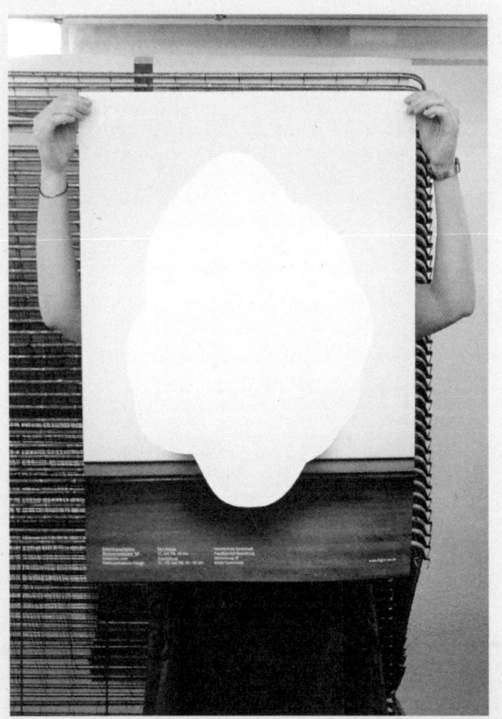

sommer
diplome
11. - 13.
juli '08

Design HOCHSCHULE DARMSTADT & PRACTISE

Client FACULTY OF DESIGN, GERMANY

Title
Dear Lulu

Specifications
Size:
150mm x 210mm, 96 pages
Colour & Print:
CMYK, digital print on demand

The book is a self-produced calibration document for testing colour, pattern, format, texture and typography when printing with print on demand, on this occasion using lulu.com.

12-13 June 2008

Dear Lulu,

Please try and print these line, colour, pattern, format, texture and typography tests for us.

Alex, Alice, André, Andreas, Anja, Christoph, Frank, James, Juliane, Michael, Patrick, Rima & Tim

Hochschule Darmstadt, FB Gestaltung
Practise, London

Red (Michael)

Orange (Alex)

Blue (Frank)

Indigo (André)

Colour Portraits ROYGBIV/White

Yellow (Tim)

Green (Juliane)

Violet (Sophie acting as Rimma)

White (Andreas)

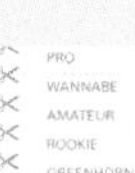

IDIOT

DRUNK

Adobe RGB (1998)

Colour Portraits (Profile / Greyscale / Halftone)

Orange (Alex)

sRGB IEC61966-2.1

CMYK (Euroscale Coated v2)

Greyscale

Halftone Screen 40lpi / 45° / Round

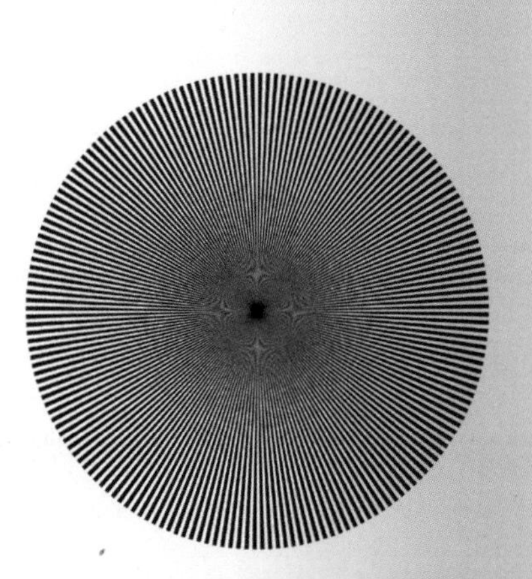

Division by one degree

Hypnosis Test

Division by five degrees

Design	Client
FORM	GOLDSMITHS, UNIVERSITY OF LONDON, UK

Title
Goldsmiths 2009/10 Undergraduate Prospectus

Specifications

Size:
250mm x 200mm, 144 pages

Colour & Print:
CMYK

Paper:
Challenger Offset, made from ECF wood pulps acquired from sustainable forest reserves

Binding:
perfect bind

Finishing:
the cover features blind-embossed panels, adding to the tactile quality while avoiding non-recyclable materials such as foil blocking or spot laminates

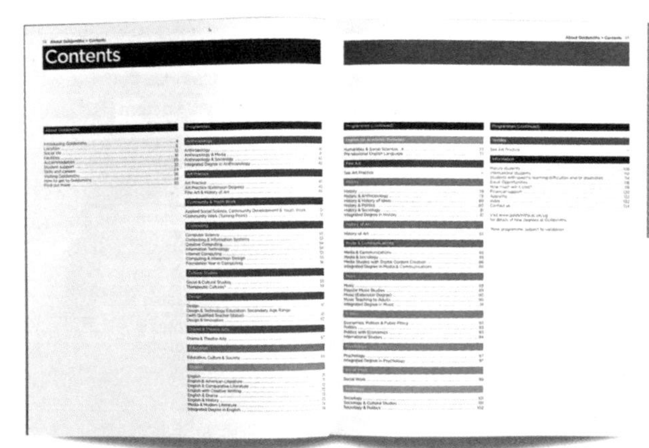
Contents

Social life
Friendly

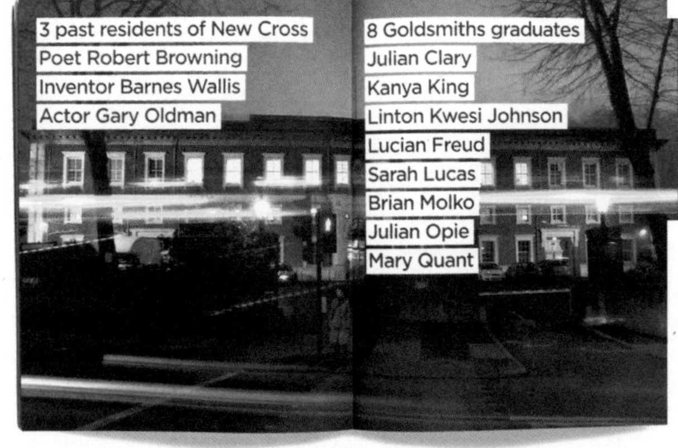
3 past residents of New Cross
Poet Robert Browning
Inventor Barnes Wallis
Actor Gary Oldman
8 Goldsmiths graduates
Julian Clary
Kanya King
Linton Kwesi Johnson
Lucian Freud
Sarah Lucas
Brian Molko
Julian Opie
Mary Quant

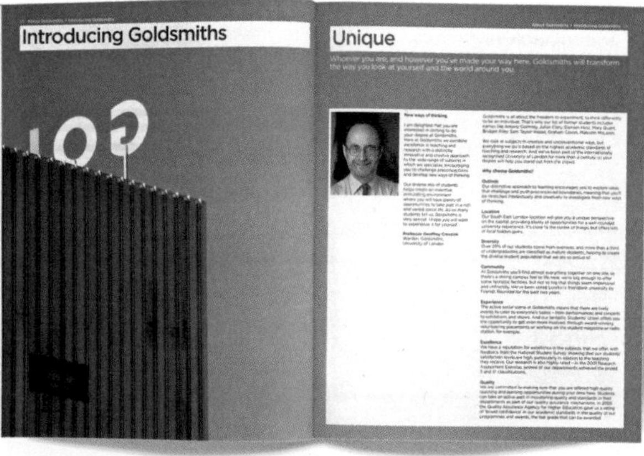
Introducing Goldsmiths
Unique

Design	**Client**
AGNES WARTNER	HGK / SCHOOL OF DESIGN, SWITZERLAND

Title
Zeit für die Bombe

Specifications
Size:
195mm x 260mm, 200 pages
Colour & Print:
1-colour (black), digital
Paper:
Medley Pure, Zanders
Binding:
swiss binding with a hard cover
Finishing:
laser cut holes

Finishing:

LASER CUT

Design	Client
VISUAL THINK	**UNIVERSITY OF UTAH, USA**

Title
What Is This?, University of Utah

Specifications

Size:
178mm x 203mm, folded
690mm x 990mm, flat
20 pages, 5 signatures, untrimmed

Colour:
front: 2-colour (fluorescent pink and black)
back: 2-colour (fluorescent orange and black)

Paper:
Fortune Matte Text, 70gsm, FSC, SFI and PEFC certified paper, which contains 10% post-consumer recycled fibre

Finishing:
user is required to trim the three edges along the dotted lines, making the document into a book

Designed in partnership with the University of Utah graphic design students. This poster teaches the reader about selecting and using typefaces and demonstrates how a book takes shape during the print production process.

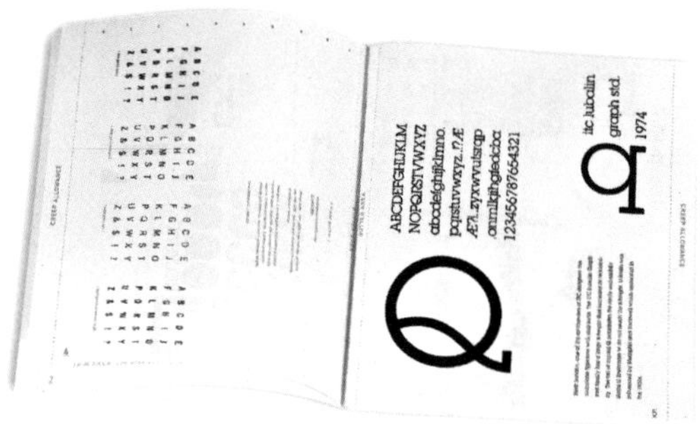

Finishing:

TRIMMING

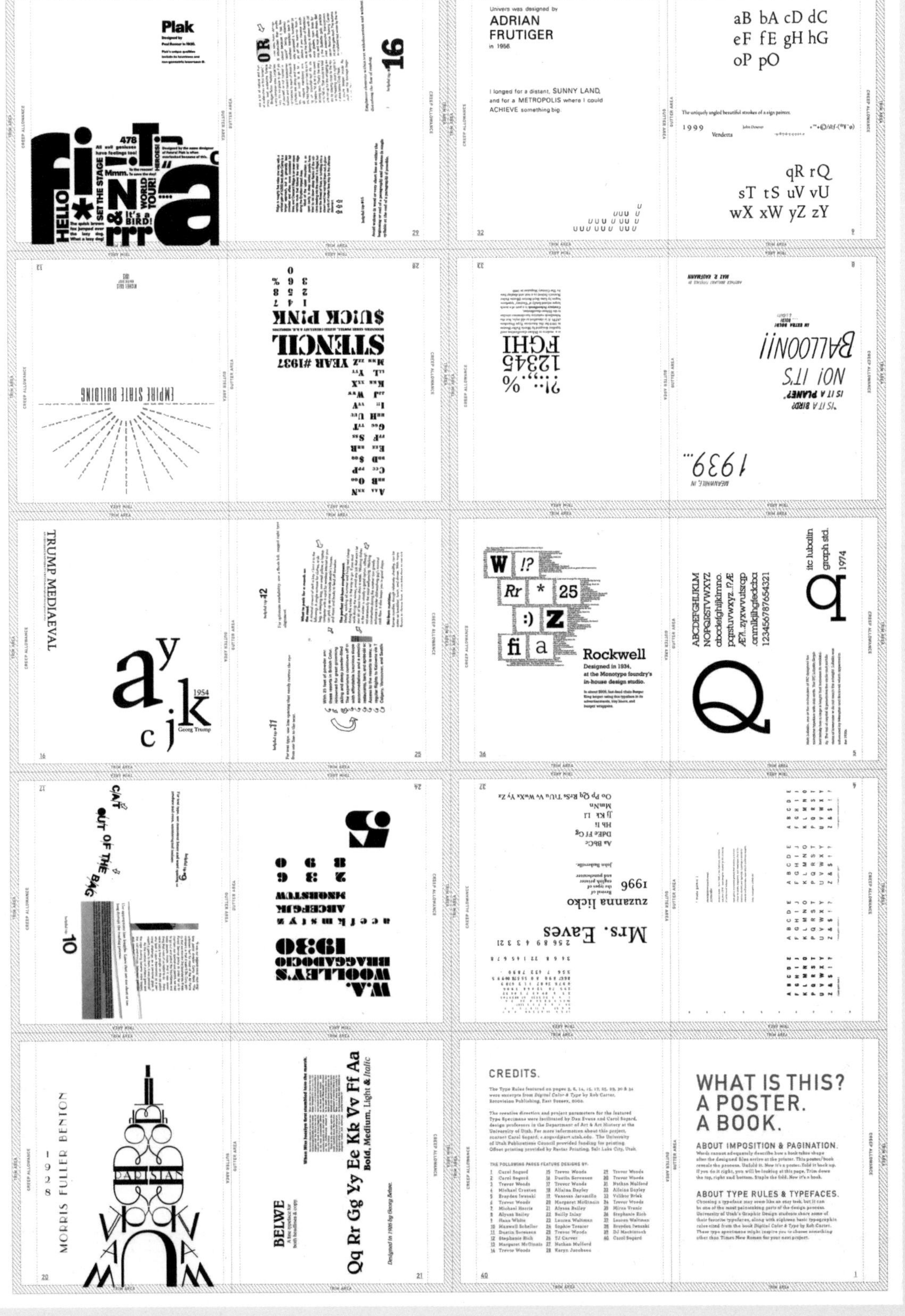

Plak
Univers was designed by
ADRIAN
FRUTIGER
in 1956.
I longed for a distant, SUNNY LAND, and for a METROPOLIS where I could ACHIEVE something big.
aB bA cD dC
eF fE gH hG
oP pO
qR rQ
sT tS uV vU
wX xW yZ zY
STENCIL
$UCK PINK
YEAR #1937
EMPIRE STATE BUILDING
BALLOON!!
NO! IT'S
1939...
TRUMP MEDIAEVAL
1954
Georg Trump
Rockwell
Designed in 1934, at the Monotype foundry's in-house design studio.
itc lubalin graph std.
1974
CAT OUT OF THE BAG
W.A. WOOLLEY'S BRAGGADOCIO 1930
Mrs. Eaves
zuzanna licko
1996
MORRIS FULLER BENTON
1928
PARISIAN
BELWE
Qq Rr Gg Yy Ee Kk Vv Ff Aa
Bold, Medium, Light & Italic
Designed in 1926 by Georg Belwe.
CREDITS.
WHAT IS THIS? A POSTER. A BOOK.
ABOUT IMPOSITION & PAGINATION.
ABOUT TYPE RULES & TYPEFACES.

Design

LUCIENNE ROBERTS +

Client

UNIVERSITIES UK, UK

Title
Annual Review 2008/09

Specifications
Size:
210mm x 250mm plus throw out from p2 measuring 185mm wide
Colour & Print:
CMYK
Paper:
cover: Revive Uncoated, 300gsm
inner pages: Revive Uncoated, 140gsm
Finishing:
index tabbed, seal throughout

Cover illustration: Clara Terne

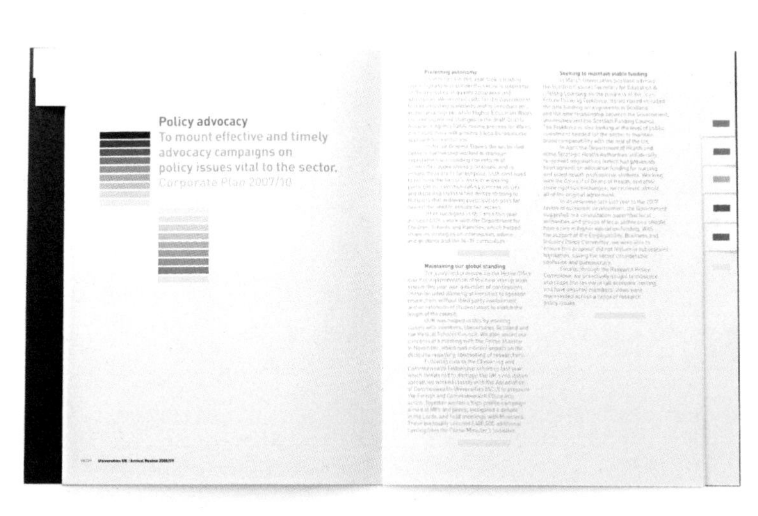

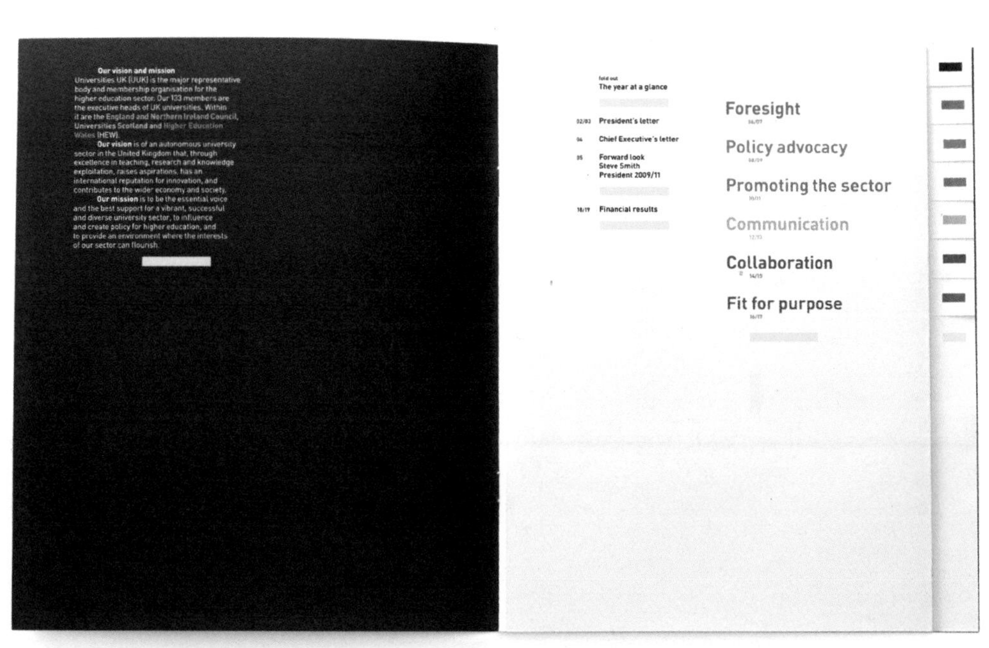
Our vision and mission
The year at a glance
President's letter
Chief Executive's letter
Forward look
Steve Smith
President 2009/11
Financial results
Foresight
Policy advocacy
Promoting the sector
Communication
Collaboration
Fit for purpose

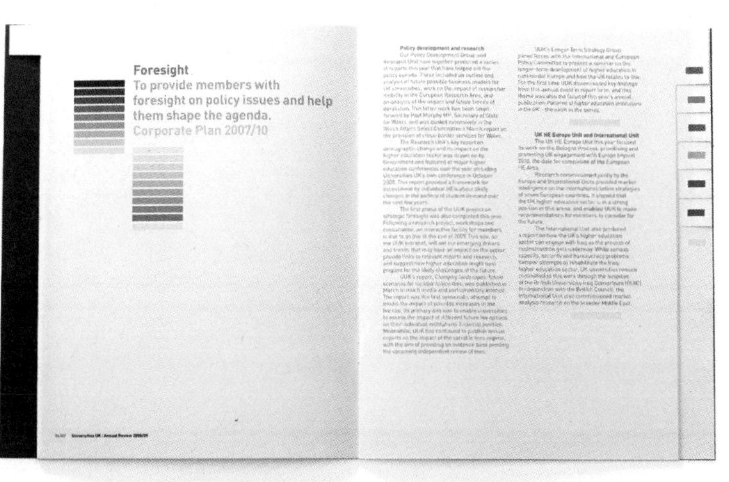
Foresight
To provide members with foresight on policy issues and help them shape the agenda.
Corporate Plan 2007/10
present a seminar on the
pment of higher education in
the UK relates to this.
eminated key findings
port form, and this
f this year's annual
er education institutions
series.
nd International Unit
nit this year focused
cess, prioritising and
with Europe beyond
n of the European

Design | **Client**

CLEVER°FRANKE | **UNIVERSITY UTRECHT, NETHERLANDS**

Title

Genome-wide Approaches Towards Identification of Susceptibility Genes in Complex Diseases

Specifications

Size:
170mm x 240mm, 176 pages

Colour:
2-colour (Pantone 805C and Pantone 8260C)

Paper:
G-Print, 135gsm, FSC certified

Folding:
the poster forms a dust-jacket

Binding:
sewn binding without hard cover

Binding:

SEWN SECTION

identification
susceptibility
in complex diseases

Genoomwijde
strategieën tot de
identificatie van
ziekte veroorza-
kende genen in
complexe ziekten

Lude Franke

anding of genetic risk as a sta
stical measure that has implica-
ions derived from a large group
of people with characteristics
equivalent to yours but does no
determine your chances for
the corresponding di

Design

Client

LUCIENNE ROBERTS +

THE UK HIGHER EDUCATION EUROPE UNIT, UK

Title
The European Higher Education Area: Celebrating a Decade of UK Engagement

Specifications
Size:
210mm x 250mm
32 pages plus 4-page cover
Colour & Print:
CMYK and 1-colour (fluorescent)
Paper:
cover: Cocoon Offset, 350gsm
inner pages: Cocoon Preprint, 140gsm
Binding:
saddle stitch using red wires
Finishing:
UV varnish on cover

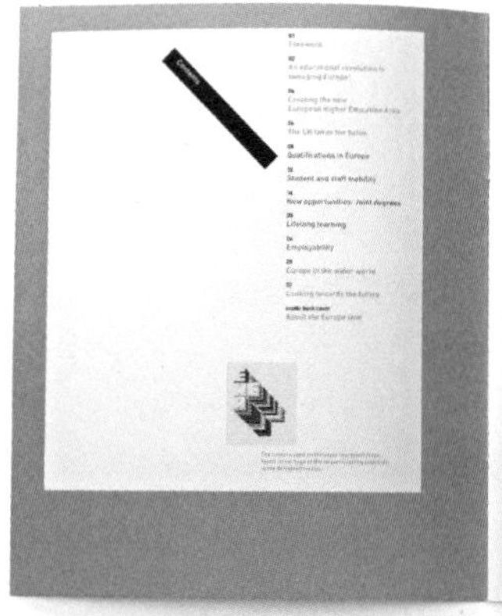

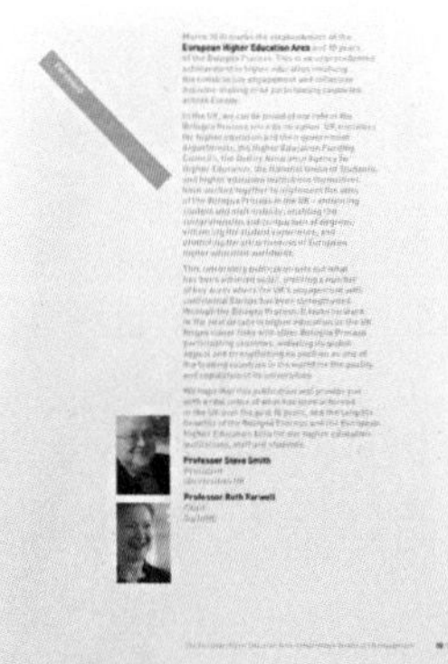

Design | Client

SOMMESE DESIGN | THE PENN STATE COLLEGE OF ARTS AND ARCHITECTURE, USA

Title
Sommese Endowment for Graphic Design Announcement

Specifications
Size:
160mm x 215mm, folded
160mm x 365mm, flat
Colour & Print:
CMYK
Paper:
Finch Fine Cover, 100gsm
Folding:
6-page accordion with extended panel

Folding:

6-PAGE ACCORDION WITH EXTENDED PANEL

Design	Client
TOBY EDWARDS, LUKE ELLIOTT, JOE STEPHENSON	NOTTINGHAM TRENT UNIVERSITY, UK

Title
Graphic Design Degree Show Invite

Specifications
Size:
130mm x 84mm
Colour & Print:
1-colour (black), silkscreen
Paper:
insert: GF Smith Colorplan Tabriz Blue, 700gsm
sleeve: GF Smith Colorplan Ebony, 120gsm
Finishing:
laser cut logo with laser engraved folds

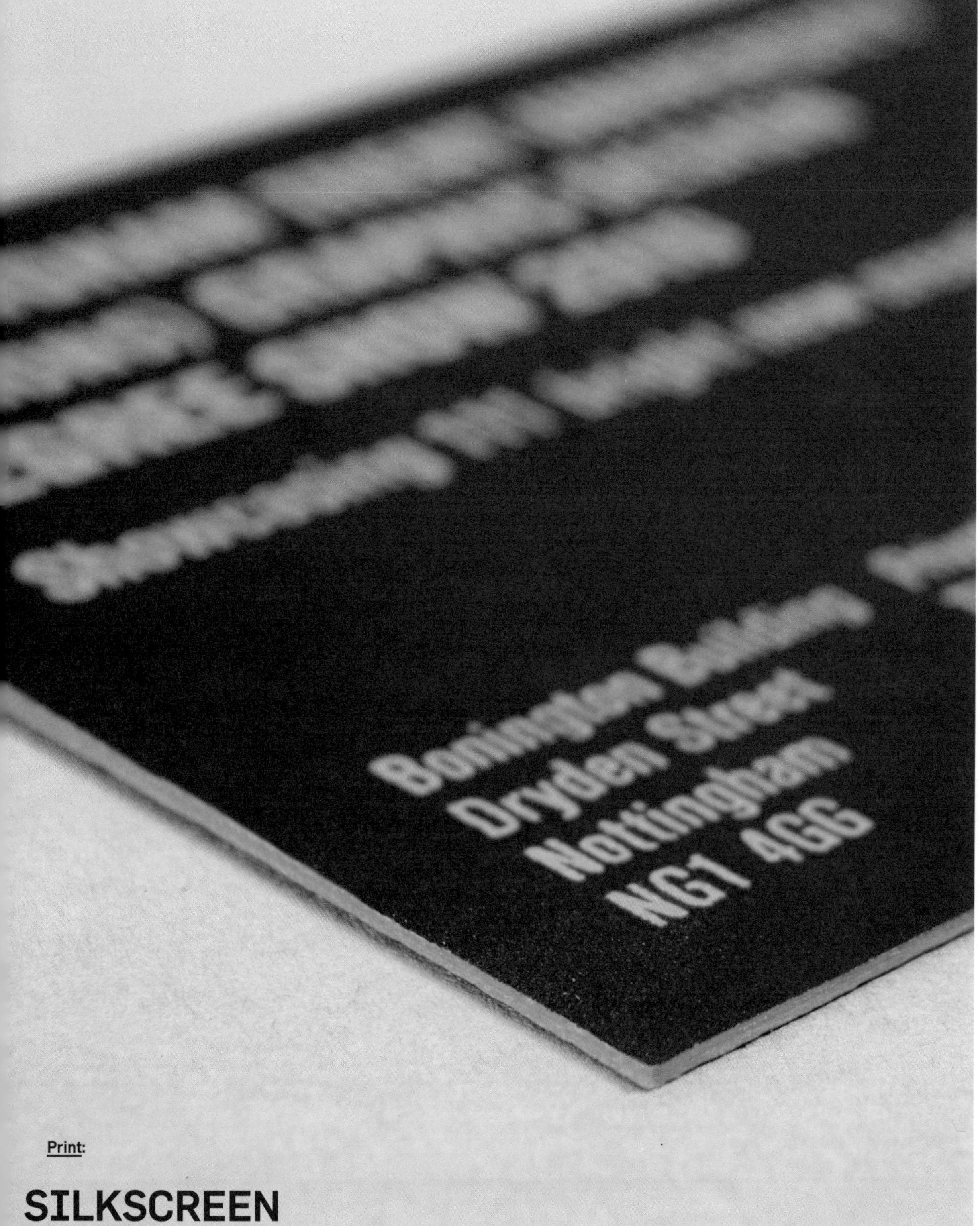

Print:

SILKSCREEN

Design | **Client**

MUELLER,WEILAND | **UNIVERSITY OF APPLIED SCIENCES DUSSELDORF, GERMANY**

Title
5 Jahre Labor Visuell

Specifications

Size:
flyer: A2 folded to A5, 16 pages
brochure: A5, 48 pages

Colour & Print:
2-colour (black and HKS-spot colour)

Paper:
BVS matt coating by Scheufelen, FSC certified
flyer: 80gsm, brochure: 150gsm

Folding:
the folded flyer also serves as a poster and as a dust jacket for the brochure

5 JAHRE
LABOR VISUELL
MIT DESIGN ÜBER
DESIGN FORSCHEN

Paper:

RECYCLED

Design | **Client**

THIS IS STUDIO | **CCW, UK**

Title
CCW Short Course Prospectuses

Specifications

Size:
165mm x 120mm
16 pages and 64 pages

Colour & Print:
16 pages: CMYK
64 pages: 2-colour
cover: 1-colour
mailer: 1-colour

Paper:
cover: Testliner 500micron
16 pages: Revive 50-50 Gloss, 150gsm
64 pages: Cyclus Offset, 115gsm
all recycled stock

Binding:
perfect bind

Finishing:
foil blocked title on the cover; a custom designed testliner mailer that houses all three prospectuses with a single spot colour sticker, measuring 60mm in diameter

CCW embodies the three college alliance of Camberwell College of Arts, Chelsea College of Art and Design and Wimbledon College of Art.

Design THIS IS STUDIO

Client MFA GOLDSMITHS, UK

Title
Goldsmiths Masters of Fine Art Catalogue

Specifications
Size:
287mm x 225mm
16 short pages
96 full-size pages
Colour & Print:
short pages: 1-colour (black)
full-size pages: CMYK
Paper:
cover: Corona Pearl Grey, 120gsm paper over 2.3mm boards
short pages: Corona Pearl Grey
full-size pages: Chromomatt, 130gsm
Binding:
casebinding with quarter bind in brillianta dark grey cloth.
Finishing:
debossed cover title, foil blocked spine title in red

Binding:

QUARTER BIND

Design

LUCIENNE ROBERTS +

Client

DESIGN MUSEUM, UK

Title

Representing Architecture
New Discussions: Ideologies, Techniques, Curation

Specifications

Size:
148mm x 200mm

Colour & Print:
cover: 1-colour (fluorescent)
pages 1-32: 1-colour
pages 33-40: CMYK
pages 41-100: 1-colour

Paper:
cover: Robert Horne Natural, 300gsm
inner pages: Robert Horne Natural, 120gsm

Finishing:
folded corners for each chapter opener

Each academic paper uses a different font designed by Adrian Frutiger, in recognition of his 80th birthday in 2008.

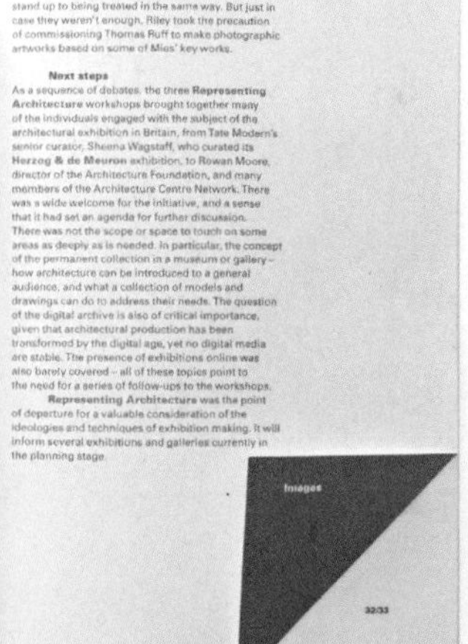

stand up to being treated in the same way. But just in case they weren't enough, Riley took the precaution of commissioning Thomas Ruff to make photographic artworks based on some of Mies' key works.

Next steps

As a sequence of debates, the three **Representing Architecture** workshops brought together many of the individuals engaged with the subject of the architectural exhibition in Britain, from Tate Modern's senior curator, Sheena Wagstaff, who curated its **Herzog & de Meuron** exhibition, to Rowan Moore, director of the Architecture Foundation, and many members of the Architecture Centre Network. There was a wide welcome for the initiative, and a sense that it had set an agenda for further discussion. There was not the scope or space to touch on some areas as deeply as is needed. In particular, the concept of the permanent collection in a museum or gallery – how architecture can be introduced to a general audience, and what a collection of models and drawings can do to address their needs. The question of the digital archive is also of critical importance, given that architectural production has been transformed by the digital age, yet no digital media are stable. The presence of exhibitions online was also barely covered – all of these topics point to the need for a series of follow-ups to the workshops.

Representing Architecture was the point of departure for a valuable consideration of the ideologies and techniques of exhibition making. It will inform several exhibitions and galleries currently in the planning stage.

Images

32/33

Introduction

Deyan Sudjic
Director
Design Museum
London

Representing Architecture
Foreword

The **Representing Architecture** workshop series explored three principal areas of concern for curators, scholars and architects in their attempts to use the exhibition as a means of communicating and disseminating architectural practice and research.

The first workshop attempted to address the underlying philosophy and the motivations that shape the representation of architecture in the museum and the gallery. The second went on to discuss the varied nature of the multiple audiences for architecture as presented in exhibition form. Finally, the third workshop focused on the purpose of architectural collections, their impact on the institutions that collect them, and their relevance for architectural exhibitions.

Each workshop brought together a range of practitioners and curators from across Britain, and also had a strong international presence. Their presentations were based on first-hand experience of the issues involved, and were designed to support continuing work in these areas.

These are themes that are being discussed in a variety of different places internationally. During the course of the three workshops, there were at least two other significant attempts to focus on the place of architecture and design in the gallery or museum context. These coincidences suggest that this is both a timely and fertile field of inquiry.

There was a synergy between these conferences. In the spring of 2007, the University of Minnesota's Design Institute, led by its director, Jan Abrams, brought together a group that included: Ole Bouman, the director of the Dutch Architecture Institute (known as the NAi) in Rotterdam, repository of the major Dutch architectural archives and collections and a pioneering example of a large-scale museum devoted to architecture; Barry Bergdoll, the chief curator of architecture and design at the
Museum

16/17

The Design Museum café, featuring **Jean Prouvé** exhibition posters by Graphic Thought Facility, 2008. Furniture by Jean Prouvé kindly loaned by Vitra.

Adrian Forty

42/43

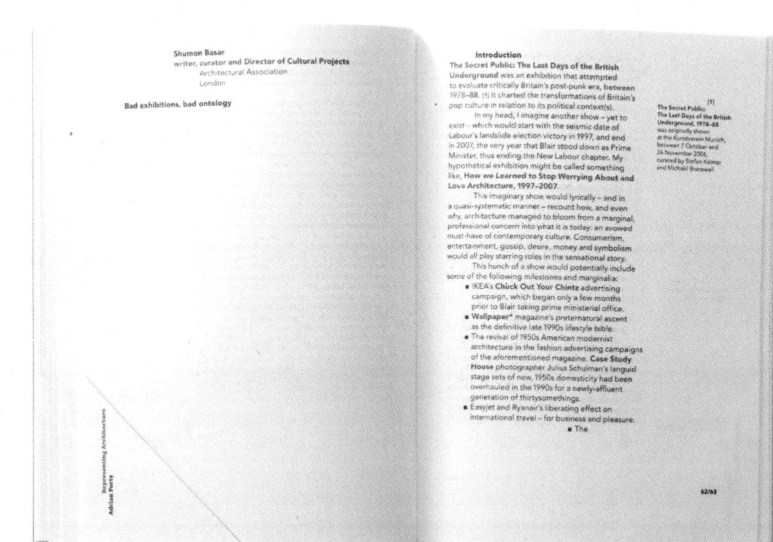

Nick Barley
Director
The Li
Scotla

Collecting and exhibiting

Representing Architecture
Peter Cachola Schmal

Design | **Client**

PATRIC SANDRI | **HSLU LUCERNE, SWITZERLAND**

Title
Degree Show Poster

Specifications
Size:
895mm x 1280mm
Colour & Print:
2-colours (black and gold), silkscreen
Paper:
biotop

:2

Chapter Two:

ARTS

Arts:

Document designs for artists and exhibitions are often the most creative briefs around. Successful case studies contain clever design solutions, reflecting the artist's work while maintaining the focus on the artist or event. A good example of this is the Longplayer Live programme leaflet by Fraser Maggeridge Studio. p. 80 The format for the 20-page, two-metre long leaflet was chosen to reflect the magnitude of the Longplayer concept: a one thousand-year long musical composition.

Limited budget can also become part of an innovative solution, like THIS IS Studio's work for the 176 Gallery. p. 98 The brief was to design a flyer for a summer exhibition 'A Tradition I Do Not Mean to Break'. The designers realised that although they had a small print budget, they could actually produce something bigger and more memorable by using postcards that were already printed for the exhibition as the images, escaping the need to print 4-colour and alleviating a bigger budget for stock and finishing processes such as die cutting.

Working with Galerie Hippolyte, Chris Bolton faced a different kind of problem – at the time of design, there were no images available. The solution was to explain the images in words; in their own manner, they reflect the artwork, leaving viewers to make their own opinions. This also allowed the whole document to be printed in one colour only. p. 74

Design

ANKER & STRIJBOS

Client

CASPAR BERGER, NETHERLANDS

Title

Update #1 Caspar Berger

Specifications

Size:
20 pages with progressive page widths

Colour & Print:
CMYK

Paper:
Arctic Volume White Plano, 170gsm

Binding:
three-hole sewn

Finishing:
brochure inserted into a custom-made sleeve

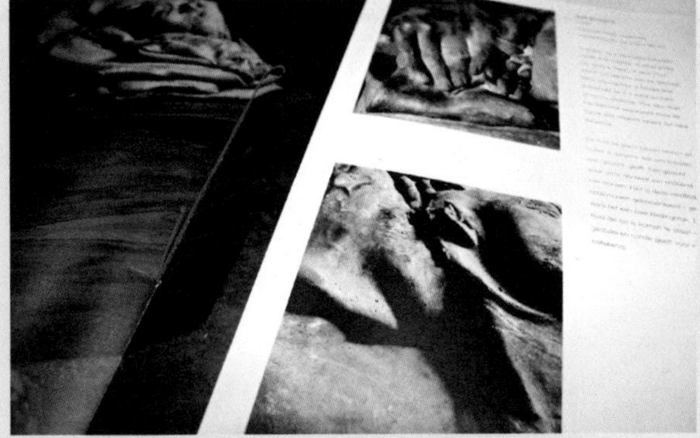

Binding:

THREE-HOLE SEWN

Design | **Client**

FRASER MUGGERIDGE STUDIO | **MILTON KEYNES GALLERY, UK**

Title
Roger Hiorns

Specifications
Size:
160 pages
Colour & Print:
cover: 1-colour (black)
inner pages: 4-colour (CMYK)/
1-colour (black)
Paper:
hardback, paper covered boards
Binding:
hardback

Printing:

4/1

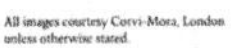

All images courtesy Corvi-Mora, London unless otherwise stated.

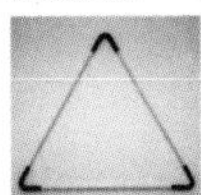

p. 17
The coming afflictions suffered for the dirt of love 2001
Metal, paint, copper sulphate
223 × 256 × 6.5cm
Private Collection

p. 18
Im Winter 2002
Galvanised steel, paint, thistles, copper sulphate
162 × 60 × 57cm
Collection of Ninah and Michael Lynne, New York

p. 19
Joy 2003
Steel, perfume (*Joy*, Jean Patou)
148 × 26 × 9cm
Courtesy Marc Foxx, Los Angeles

p. 20
L'heure bleue 2003
Steel, perfume (*L'Heure Bleue*, Guerlain)
145.5 × 26 × 9cm
Private Collection
Courtesy Galerie Nathalie Obadia, Paris

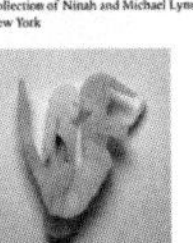

p. 21
The pleasure received in pain 2003
Alabaster, carbon
25.5 × 20 × 6cm
Collection of Konstantinos Papageorgiou, Athens

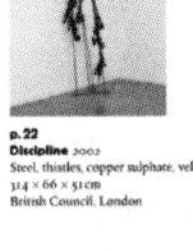

p. 22
Discipline 2002
Steel, thistles, copper sulphate, velcro
314 × 66 × 51cm
British Council, London

p. 23
Come with me to the forest it's dark now and everyone will be gone we'll walk gently through the gates of joy and see the birth of the rare bird 2001
Oak
168 × 192 × 6cm
Collection of Konstantinos Papageorgiou, Athens

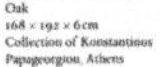

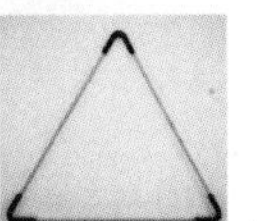

p. 26
Weakness 2003
Metal, paint, copper sulphate
230 × 280 × 6.5cm
Collection of Alice Kosmin, New York

p. 27
Working out for It's They Me Or The Red Hawthorne Tree
2001
Pencil on paper, framed
55 × 63.5 × 3cm

pp. 28–29
The heart has its own reasons 2002
Stainless steel, nylon
162 × 214 × 60.5cm
Private Collection

p. 30
Creed 2003
Steel, perfume (*Fleurs de Bulgarie*, Creed)
134 × 26 × 9.5cm

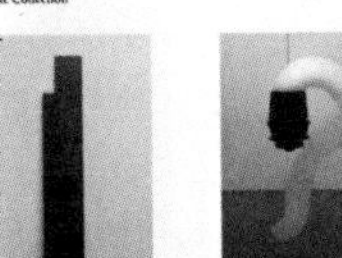

p. 31
Vauxhall 2003
Steel, perfume (*First*, Van Cleef & Arpels)
134 × 26 × 9.5cm
Private Collection

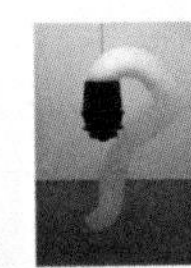

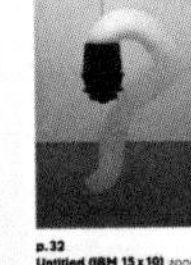

p. 32
Untitled (IBM 15 x 10) 2000
Ceramic, plastic, compressor, foam
30 × 23cm
Private Collection

p. 33
Temporary construction to hidden obligations 2001
Steel, enamel, nylon
162 × 214 × 60.5cm
Private Collection

p. 34
Weakness 2004
Bronze
23 × 18.5 × 6.5cm
Edition of nine and two artist's proofs
Various private collections

p. 35
Routine 2005
Cardboard, resin
70 × 48 × 13cm

p. 37
L'instant 2004
Steel, perfume (*L'Instant*, Guerlain)
147.5 × 26 × 9cm
Collection of Oliver Ferreira, New York

147

Come with me to the forest it's dark now and everyone will be gone we'll walk gently through the gates of joy and see the birth of the rare bird 2001

Discipline 2002

23

Design

UNFOLDED

Client

KUNSTHOF ZÜRICH, SWITZERLAND

Title
Invasionswetterlage

Specifications

Size:
148mm x 210mm

Colour & Print:
cover: 1-colour (white), silkscreen
inner pages: 1-colour (black)

Paper:
Plano Color (black, yellow, red), 80gsm and 160gsm

Binding:
saddle stitch

Binding:

SADDLE STITCH

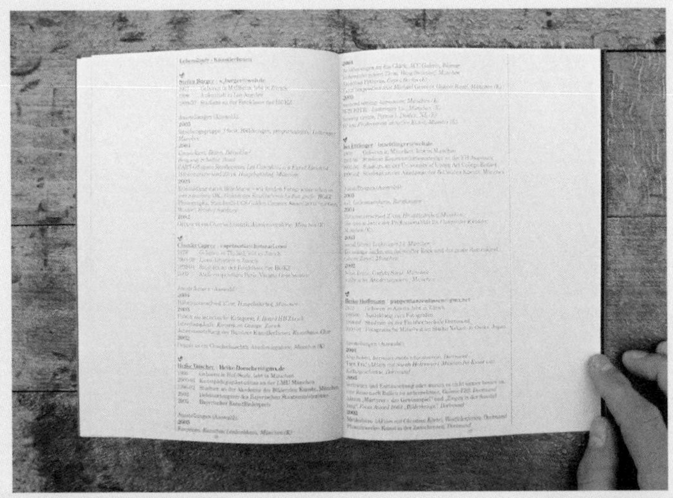

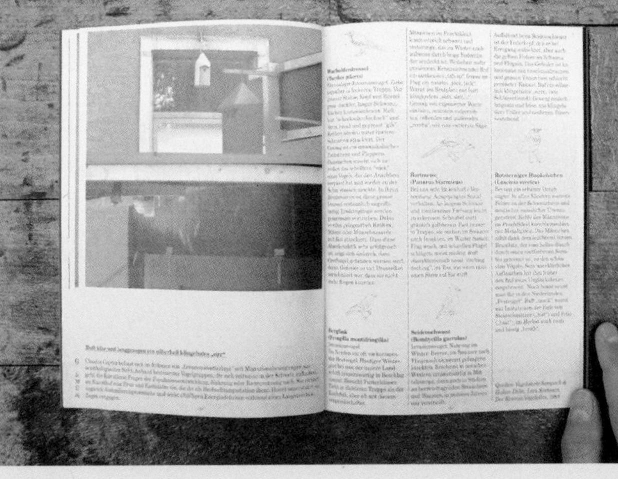

Design **Client**

CHRIS BOLTON **GALERIE HIPPOLYTE, FINLAND**

Title
An Exhibition Curated by a Very Important Curator

Specifications
Size:
A6, 16 pages
Colour:
2-colour
Paper:
Munken Lynx, FSC certified
Binding:
saddle stitch

At the time of design, there were no digital images available. The solution was to explain the images in words. In their own manner, the words reflect the artwork, leaving viewers to make their own opinions.

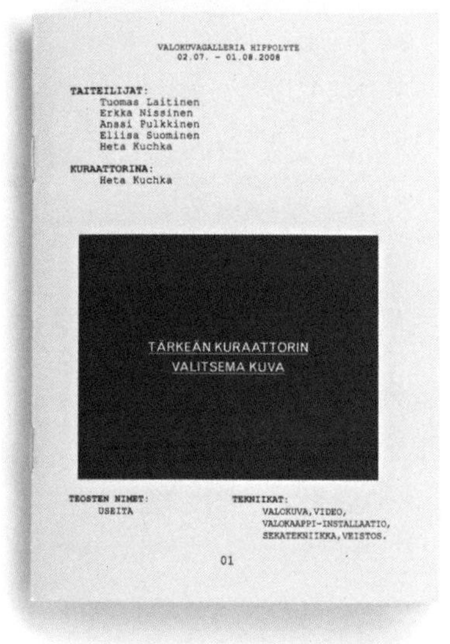

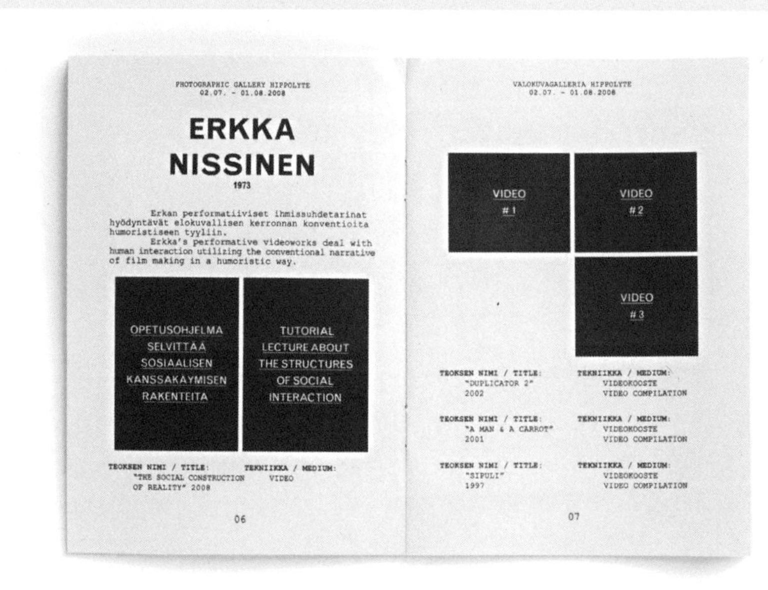

ckivat
ivihkaa
ikkeiden

agination
llows
ace of

STALLAATIO

VALOKUVAGALLERIA HIPPOLYTE
02.07. - 01.08.2008

A DRUNKEN MAN IS SWAYING
IN FRONT OF THE MIRROR
YOU CAN HEAR THE SOUND OF A
MOTOR IN THE BACKGROUND

TITLE:
FROM THE SERIES
"BREATHE" 2008

MEDIUM:
LIGHT BOX INSTALLATION

05

Design **Client**

CHRIS BOLTON **HELSINKI CITY ART MUSEUM, FINLAND**

Title
Yours Truly

Specifications
Size:
250mm x 250mm, 36 pages
Colour & Print:
CMYK plus 1-colour (gold) on cover
Paper:
Galerie Silk, FSC certified
Binding:
section sewn
Finishing:
die-cut cover

Design	Client
BRUKETA&ZINIC OM	ABUS, CROATIA

Title
The Book of Genesis

Specifications
Size:
210mm x 270mm, 400 pages
Colour & Print:
CMYK
Paper:
cover: artificial leather
inner pages: Munken Pure, 150gsm
Finishing:
die-cut circle on 112 pages holds a CD; two silk ribbon bookmarks are bound into the book at the top of the spine

Knjiga
Postanka

Design

Client

FRASER MUGGERIDGE STUDIO

THE LONGPLAYER TRUST, UK

Title
Jem Finer, Longplayer
Live Programme

Specifications
Size:
2m long, 20 pages
Colour:
1-colour (black)
Paper:
brown packaging paper
Folding:
concertina fold, joined with blue binding tape as the format was too long to make from one single sheet

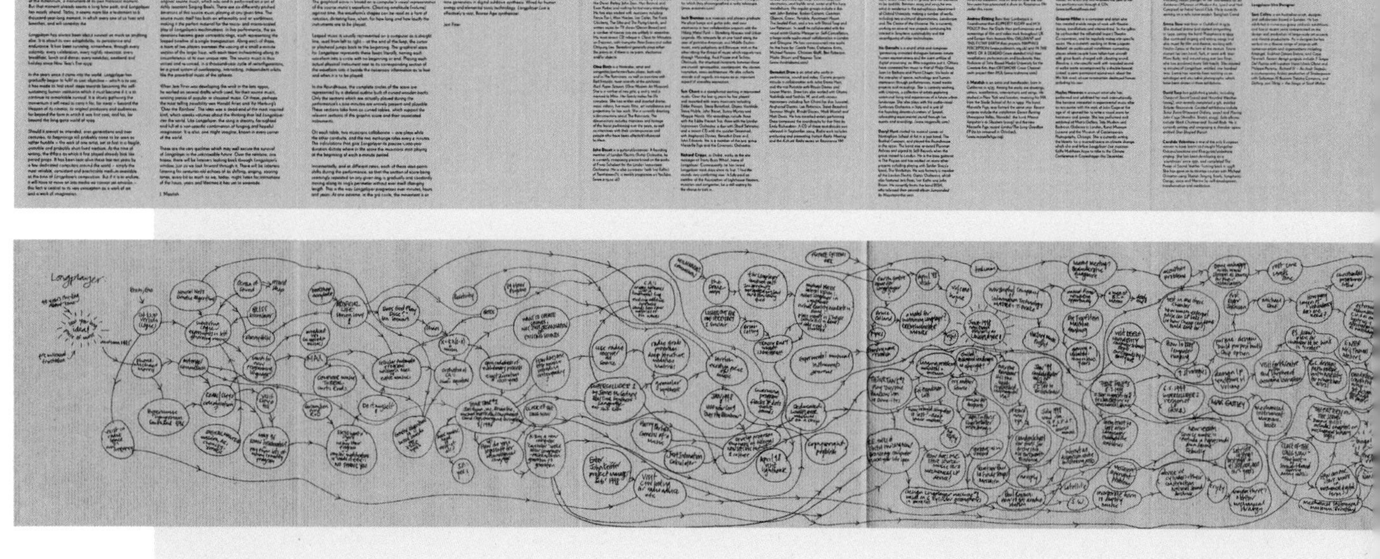

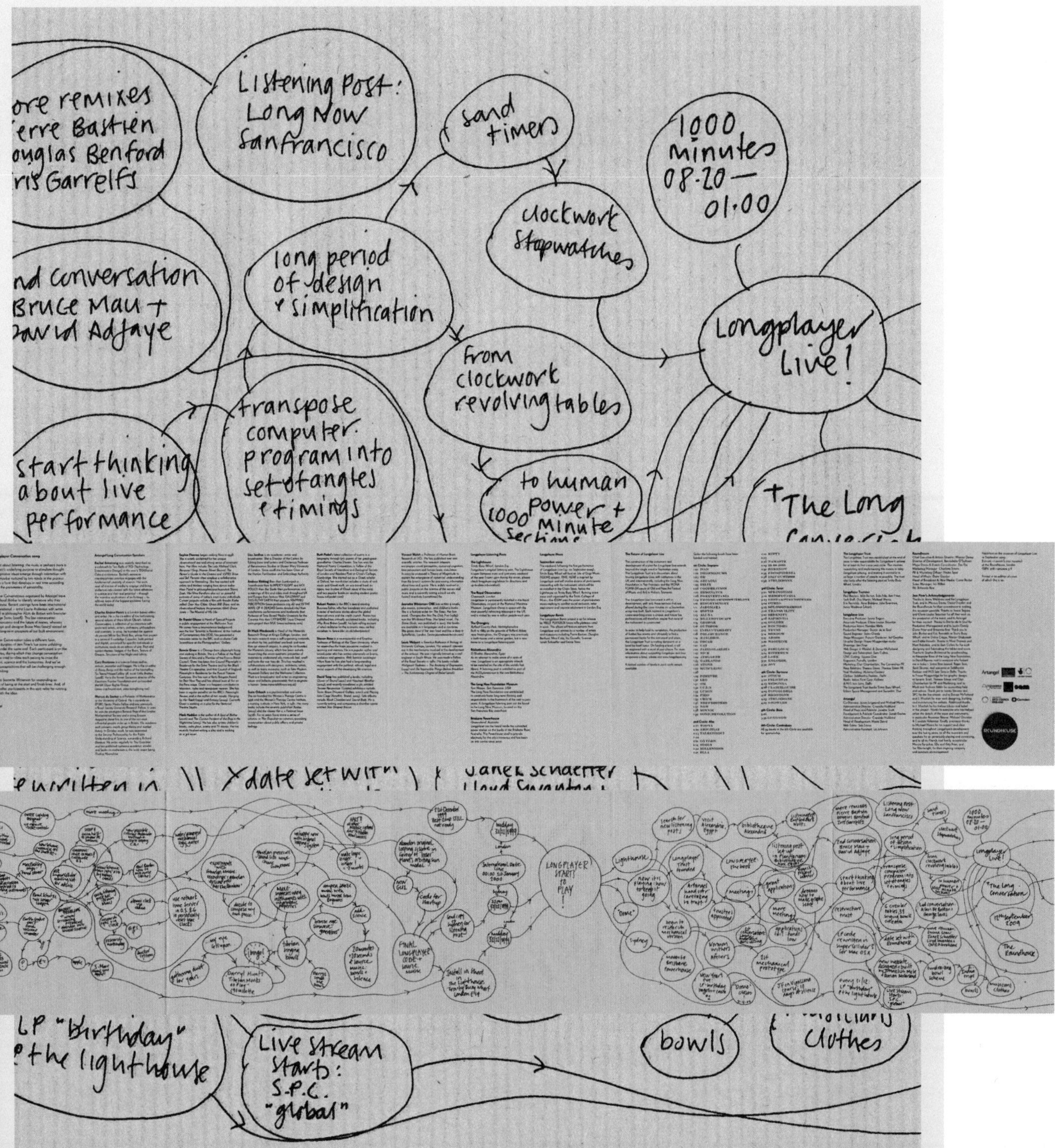

Listening Post: Long Now San Francisco
sand timers
1000 minutes 08·20— 01·00
clockwork stopwatches
long period of design + simplification
Longplayer Live!
from clockwork revolving tables
transpose computer program into set of angles + timings
start thinking about live performance
to human power + 1000 minute sections
bowls
clothes
Live stream starts: S.P.C. "global"

Design

CHRIS BOLTON

Client

GALERIE HEINO, FINLAND

Title
In Memory of...

Specifications
Size:
175mm x 230mm, 32 pages
Colour & Print:
cover: 1-colour
inner pages: CMYK
Paper:
cover: recycled board
inner pages: Galerie Silk
Binding:
section sewn with black-cloth spine, affixed front and back covers

TUOMO
&
PAAVO
12
13

22
23

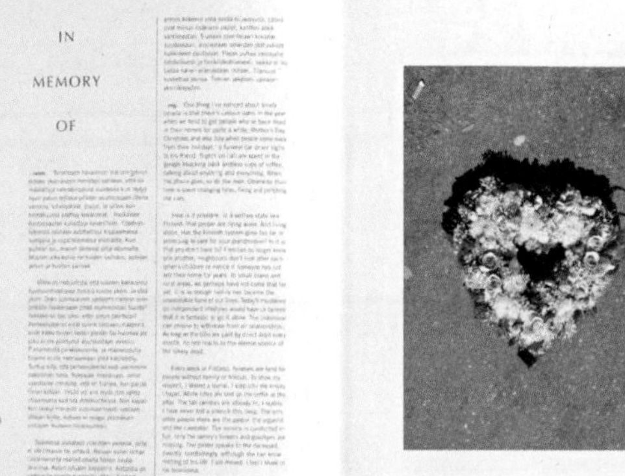
IN
MEMORY
OF
04
05

Design

Client

CHRIS BOLTON

KIASMA, HELSINKI

Title
Drawn in the Clouds

Specifications
Size:
195mm x 265mm, 64 pages
Colour & Print:
section 1: 2-colour
section 2: CMYK
Paper:
Munken Lynx (uncoated stock used for Texts section) and Galerie Art Silk (contrasting coated stock used for Image section), FSC certified
Binding:
casebinding
Finishing:
silver foil blocking on cover

Finishing:

FOIL BLOCKING

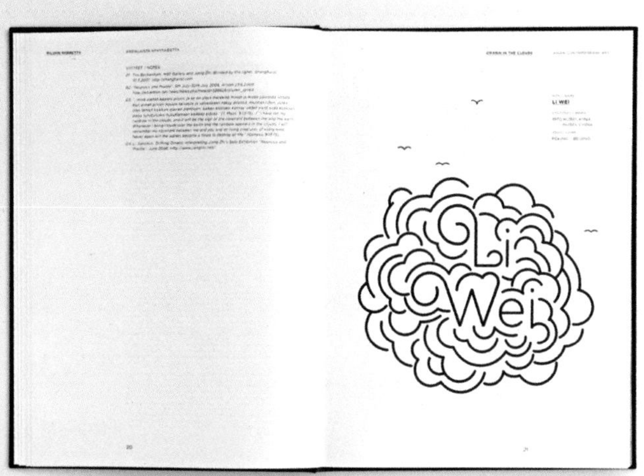
Li Wei

Pilviin pirretty
KIASMA

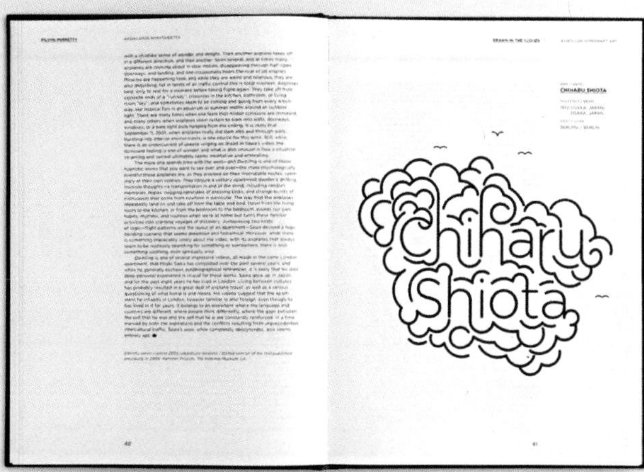
Chiharu Shiota

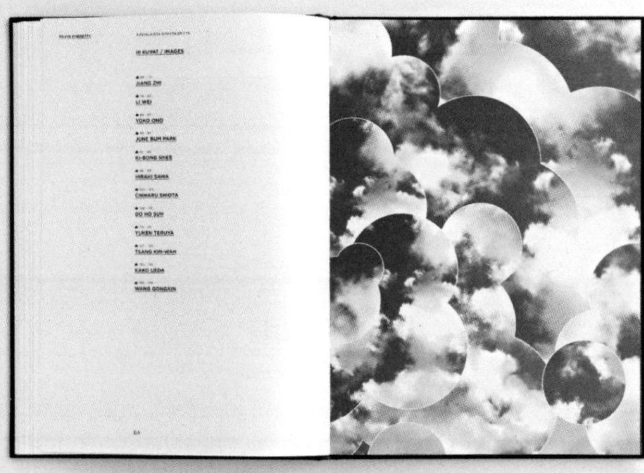

Design | **Client**

ISABEL VAN DER VELDEN | ROYAL ACADEMY OF ART, THE HAGUE, THE NETHERLANDS

Title
First Aid for Design

Specifications

Size:
125mm x 175mm, 32 pages

Colour:
1-colour (black)

Paper:
four types of coloured paper stock, 200gsm

Binding:
perfect bind

Finishing:
four black ribbon bookmarks bound into the book at the top of the spine

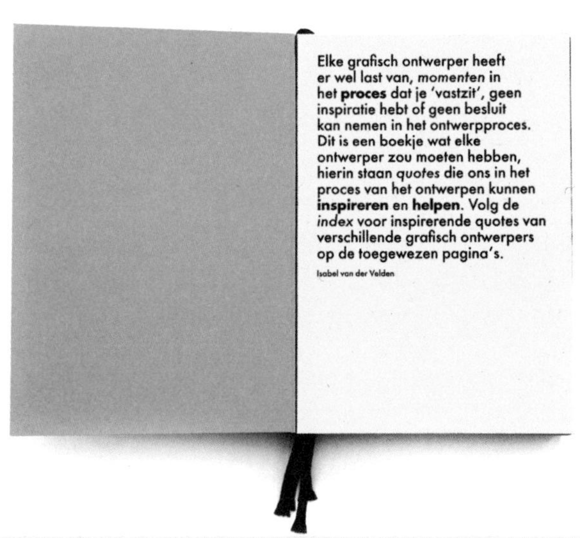

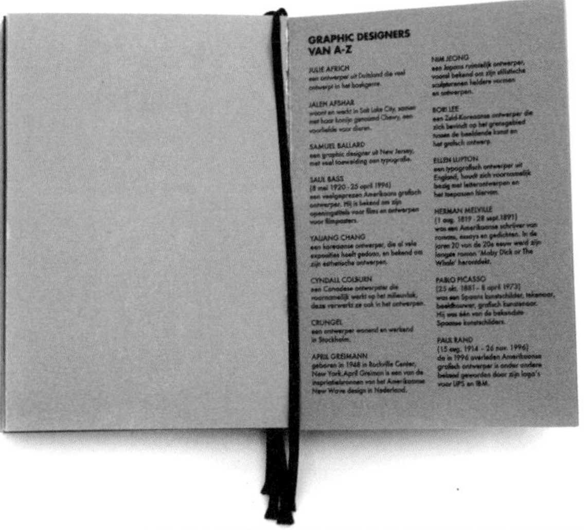

EERSTE HULP BIJ ONTWERPEN

Design	Client
DESIGN AGENCY TANGO	THE ASSOCIATION OF FINNISH SCULPTORS, FINLAND

Title
100 Years, The Association of Finnish Sculptors

Specifications

Size:
poster: 350mm x 700mm
brochure, folded, two sided: 297mm x 420mm
envelopes: A4 and A5

Colour:
2-colour (Pantone 872 and black)

Paper:
Munken Polar

Folding:
brochure: 8-page accordion

Finishing:
blind embossing

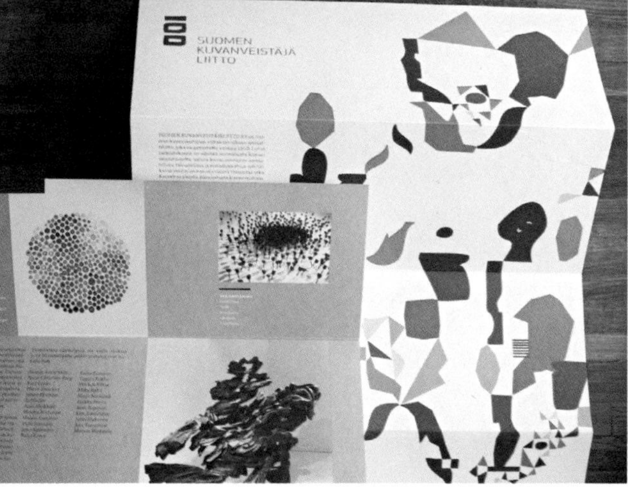

Design HUDSON-POWELL

Client 176/ZABLUDOWICZ COLLECTION, UK

Title
Matt Stokes / The Gainsborough Packet, &c.

Specifications

Size:
148mm x210mm, 76 pages plus 4-page cover

Colour & Print:
CMYK plus 1-colour

Paper:
Starline Kraftback, Munken Print White, Munken Print Cream, Maxigloss, Clairefontanie Pink

Binding:
section sewn

Finishing:
embossed cover

THE GAINSBOROUGH PACKET, &C.
Matt Stokes

ZABLUDOWICZ COLLECTION

CONTENTS

/1,000

stimulus to recount moments of recollection to another person suffers from arbitrary impulsiveness.

The storyteller, as we ALL are in our everyday narration of life, chooses not only the epic; the smallest act once out in the public domain is described and retold, altered and eventually re-circled back, rarely in its original form. These stories are invoked over generations and are in constant states of transformation. It is the minutiae of another's life and of its comparison to our own that fascinate us most.

The CONVINCING tale is one seemingly unpolished and unpractised. Falsehood might only be detected in an over-confidently pronounced phrase, conspicuous repetition, or a lazy disengaged tone. Once the story is caught out, the disappointed listener retreats and the trade is over. Belief is dashed.

Not a trace of doubt in my mind.[‡]

Balances waver precariously within conversations already fraught with disputed weights. Better to begin with open mind as the everyday encounter accommodates the small incisions of exchange, where commonality and discord find their respective levels.

I'm a Believer.[§]

[*] Lyric from PSYCHO KILLER written by David Byrne, Talking Heads, 1977
[†] Didion, Joan. THE WHITE ALBUM (London: Flamingo), 1995
[‡] Lyric from I'M A BELIEVER written by Neil Diamond, 1966
[§] Title lyric from I'M A BELIEVER written by Neil Diamond, 1966

82

THE BALLAD OF BRITAIN

an ancient memory," she said, before embarking on the most spine-chilling version of *Willie O'Winsbury* I have ever heard.

Is folk music still relevant? I would say that it most certainly is, as long as it is accepted as an organic, ever-changing form that cannot be contained within the strictures of dogma. There's nothing better than standing in a pub with people singing all around you, and the real value of the music is its egalitarianism: there's a strong feeling of community that comes from singing songs that stretch deep into the past and that, with their universal themes of love, betrayal, hardship and mystery, belong to the present — and to all of us.

To some extent, folk music does belong to a subculture. It remains outside of the mainstream and has its own community, although perhaps not the one of popular cliché (bearded men smelling faintly of wee). And its great strength is the fact that it can't be captured. It's rather like a butterfly. It is only beautiful, it only has value, when it is flying free. Pin it down and you render it lifeless.

32

THE GAINSBOROUGH PACKET
Lyrics by Jon Boden

◆◆◆◆◆◆◆◆◆◆◆

[I]
I cannot write a history all of my life in full
But just such things that happened to me here in Newcastle
On the fifth day of October, Seventeen hundred and Ninety Six
Now what think you of this, my friend Pybus?
To the church of All Saints' steeple, up to the very top
My comrades then invited me to climb
Being strong in nerve and muscle I granted them their wish
Now what think you of this, my friend Pybus?

Oh what think you of this?
Are we blown by fortune's wind?
Or does the Lord ordain all things to try us?
But man impoverished is
If he a single moment miss
Now what think you of this, my friend Pybus?

68

[II]
I had not long been settled in old Newcastle town
One day as I was walking by the Tyne
A girl upon the dockside played, but then her footing missed
Now what think you of this, my friend Pybus?
So taking off my hat and watch into the stream I dived
I swam like Zeus to save her from the tide
But when we to dry land returned my hat and watch I missed
Now what think you of this, my friend Pybus?

Oh what think you of this?
Are we blown by fortune's wind?
Or does the Lord ordain all things to try us?
A man may lose his hat
Just to save a drowning brat
Now what think you of that, my friend Pybus?

[III]
But being of a courage bold a fireman I became
And many's the inferno I have braved
On board the Gainsborough Packet my very life I risked
Now what think you of this, my friend Pybus?
Down in the smoke-filled cabin, with powder I was trapped
The fire it raged, the smoke it filled my lungs
Before the waters took me I escaped from fortune's tryst
Now what think you of this, my friend Pybus?

Oh what think you of this?
Are we blown by fortune's wind?

69

Design	Client
JULIA	PAGE TSOU, UK

Title
Page Tsou

Specifications
Size:
closed: 115mm x 200mm
open: 329mm x 483mm
Colour & Print:
cover: 1-colour (black), laser
inner pages: 1-colour (black), risograph
Paper:
cover: Folders Buff Paper
inner pages: Paperback Corona Offset, 130gsm
Binding:
swiss binding

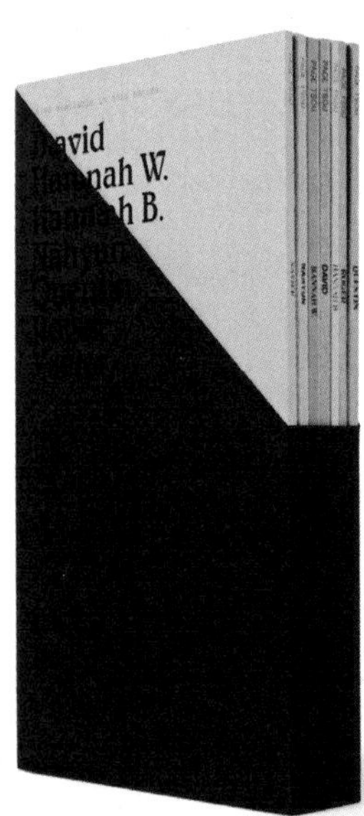

PAGE TSOU QUENTIN
PAGE TSOU ROGER
PAGE TSOU HANNAH B.
PAGE TSOU DAVID
PAGE TSOU HANNAH W.
PAGE TSOU NAHYUN
PAGE TSOU XAVIER

Design

FRASER MUGGERIDGE STUDIO

Client

BEACON ART PROJECT, UK

Title

Kelly Large, Our Name Is Legion

Specifications

Size:
16 pages plus 4-page cover

Colour & Print:
cover: 1-colour (fluorescent)
inner pages: 12 pages printed 1-colour (black) and wrapped around a 4-page (CMYK) middle section

Binding:
saddle-stitch

Foreword

It has been fascinating to witness the gestation of Kelly Large's project, *Our Name is Legion*, over the last few months. Kelly was given a deliberately loose brief as to what was expected of her when she was commissioned to work with the students of Kesteven and Sleaford High School. None of the participants, the school, Beacon or Kelly knew what the outcome of the commission would be. The starting point of the project was an act of faith from all those involved and as with a lot of things the key is in the detail. This is certainly true in the case of a process-led project such as this, in which the processes employed by Kelly when developing the project have had a generative effect, extending the life of the project beyond the initial terms of engagement from the residency to the event, the filming, the editing, the screening, the panel discussion and now this publication. The image on pages 8 and 9 taken on the day of the event, frames a discursive arena in which each of the three texts offers us a perspective of a distinct aspect of the project, the process, the film itself and the wider cultural implications. This publication is one of a range of outcomes that form the expanded project of *Our Name is Legion*, and I look forward to future developments.

John Plowman

2

Our Name is Legion

We are looking down upon a town centre street. In the camera's eye is a slow moving lane of traffic, a high street bank and a bin lorry is moving sluggishly along. School children move up and down, their bags heavy upon their backs. They wear dark blazers, the girls wear black trousers or short skirts and the boys are growing tall like bean shoots, all gangly and thin.

Suddenly, three abreast come other teenagers: in luminescent yellow safety vests and then emptiness. The street is momentarily still. Then quickly there are more, seven, ten, fifteen... thirty – they are pouring towards us, disappearing beneath the camera, a swarm of garish, fluorescent yellow.

I try to remember what it was like, when twisting the uniform felt edgy, rebellious and individual. I can't. They are a strange alien generation.

Our Name is Legion

Daniel Defoe famously used this quote from Mark's gospel (5:9) to sign on behalf of the petitioners, in his 'Legion's Address to the Lords'. In doing so, not only did he claim to speak on behalf of innumerable commoners but he also invoked a spirit of revolution.

Our Name is Legion

We are looking into a schoolyard, it is completely empty. Through the classroom windows there are moving shadows. A boy comes out, wearing a hi-vis vest and carrying a black jacket. He lifts his arms into the air as he walks and slowly twirls, aware of the camera, perhaps not sure where it is – so twirling for all watchers.

The town square gradually fills. It is stationary but moving, a constant flow of chatting, moving teenagers. Among the growing

3

Design | **Client**

344 DESIGN, LLC | **L.A. LOUVER, USA**

Title

Rogue Wave Catalogue

Specifications

Size:
12" x 7" with a 12° angle cut on the fore edge, 80 pages

Colour & Print:
CMYK
center section: CMYK plus 1-colour (PMS grey)

Paper:
FSC certified

Binding:
perfect bind

Finishing:
spot gloss varnish on both covers

The book works from both sides to give both shows equal coverage. The introduction is at the center and the pages flow out towards the covers in alphabetical order.

Design	**Client**
DAN ALEXANDER & CO	ERETZ ISRAEL MUSEUM, ISRAEL

Title
Itay Noy, A Second Second

Specifications
Size:
A4
Colour & Print:
inner pages: CMYK plus metallic spot colour
Paper:
cover: leather-like paper stock
Binding:
section sewn, hard back
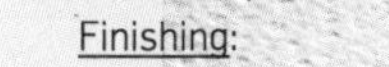
Finishing:
embossed cover

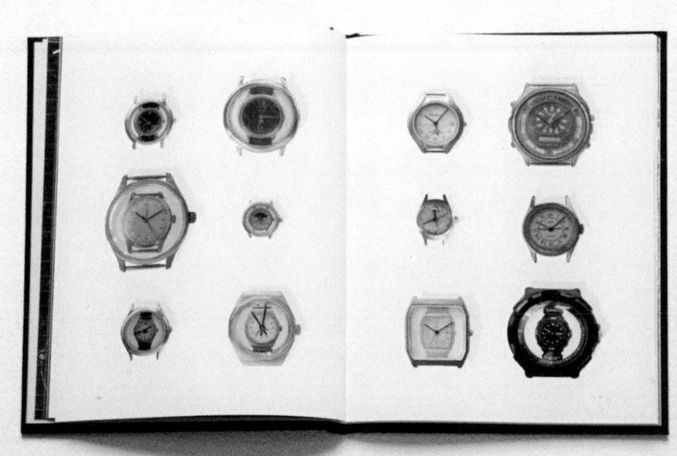

TimePieces

Design	Client
THIS IS STUDIO	176 GALLERY, UK

Title
A Tradition I Do Not Mean to Break

Specifications
Size:
210mm x 140mm
Colour & Print:
1-colour (Pantone)
Paper:
Cairn Natural Cream, 320gsm, 100% recycled
Finishing:
10-page concertina fold with die cuts

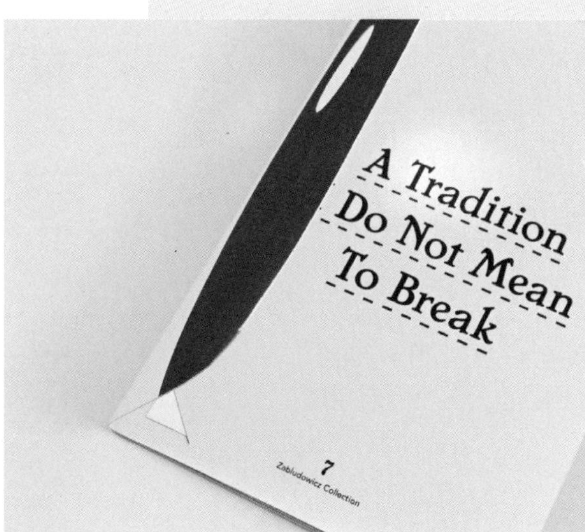

Format:

CONCERTINA

Design

RE-PUBLIC

Client

JONAS LIVERÖD, DENMARK

Title

The Violence

Specifications

Size:
230mm x 335mm, 200 pages

Colour & Print:
2-colour (Pantone black overprint and Pantone 7506), silkscreen

Paper:
front and back sections: Scandia 2000, 150gsm
The violent Altamont section from California 1969: Bible paper, 60gsm
Jonas's artwork section: Scandia 2000, 130gsm

Binding:
open-spine and thread-sewn binding

Finishing:
spot varnish; rounded corners; 700 copies signed by the artist

Binding:

OPEN SPINE

PROPERTY OF
JONAS LIVERÖD
SUBJECT:
THE VIOLENCE
GROWING UP AND COMING DOWN
THE VIOLENCE

Design

VTJE890 ONTWERPERS

Client

ZUIDERZEE MUSEUM, NETHERLANDS

Title
Monument / Clare Twomey

Specifications

Size:
160mm x 240mm, 40 pages

Colour & Print:
CMYK

Paper:
Biotop, 150gsm

Binding:
thread-sewn section

Finishing:
embossed cover; each inner page perforated

Finishing:

PERFORATION

Design | **Client**

.JULTA | FEDERICO GALLO, UK

Title
Order

Specifications
Size:
230mm x 300mm, 70 pages
Print:
digital
Paper:
cover: HP Photo Paper, 300gsm
inner pages: Digital Uncoated, 120gsm
Binding:
french fold

With bespoke typography.

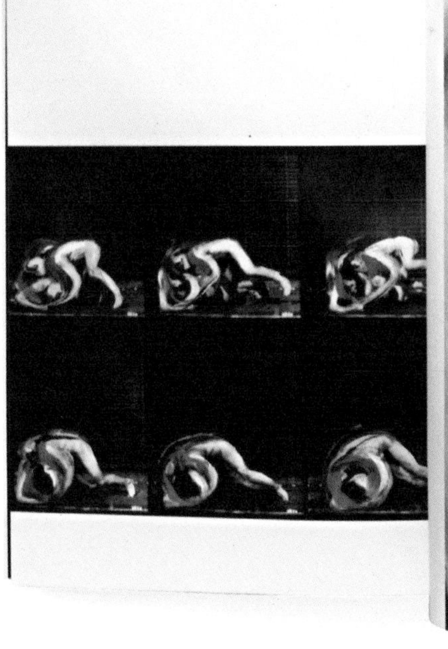

Format:

FRENCH FOLD

ORDER

Design

STUDIO BAER

Client

HOST GALLERY, UK

Title
Maurice Broomfield Monograph

Specifications
Size:
200mm x 254mm, 128 pages
Colour & Print:
CMYK
Paper:
book: pristine white heavy-weight paper with black uncoated endpapers
box: light-grey uncoated paper stock
Binding:
thread-sewn section
Finishing:
a limited edition of 100 signed and numbered books are presented in a custom-made portfolio case with an accompanying signed silver gelatin print

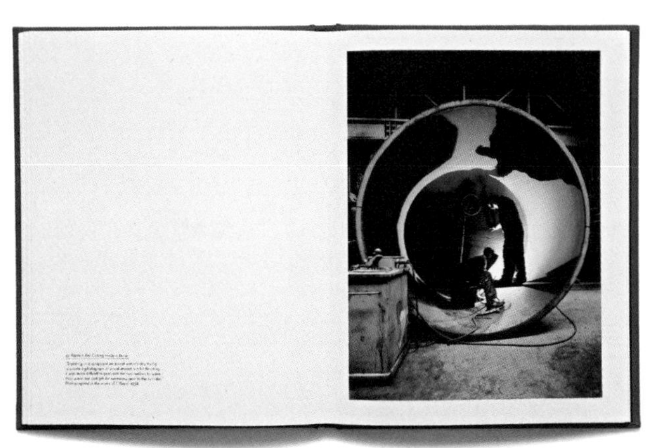

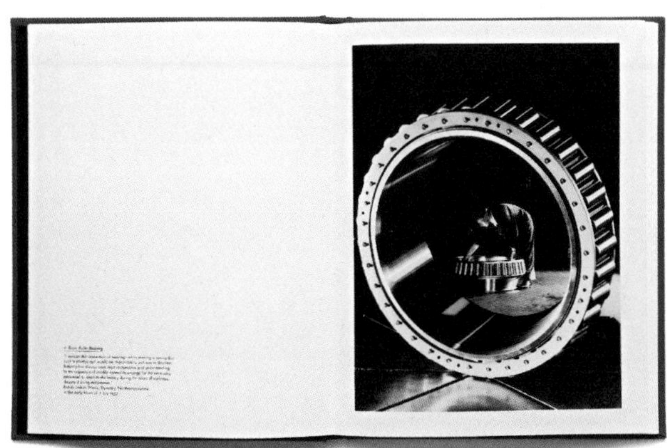

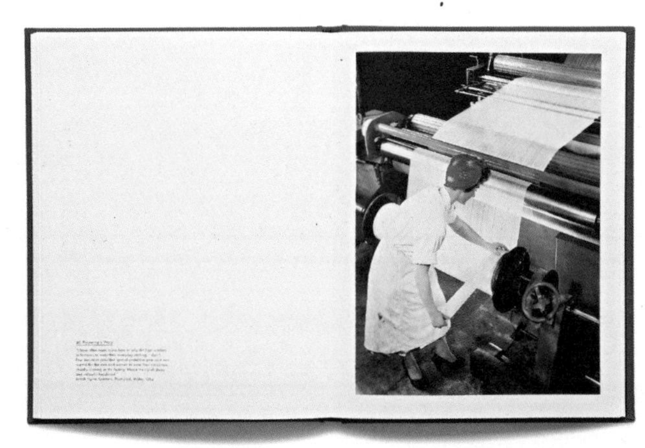

Design

SARAH BORIS

Client

THE INSTITUTE OF CONTEMPORARY ARTS, UK

Title
ICA Monthly Guide

Specifications
Size:
A5, an average of 32 pages
Colour & Print:
1-colour (black), litho
Paper:
Challenger, 70gsm, FSC certified virgin fibre content, sourced from well-managed and sustainable forests
Binding:
saddle stitch

Font: Theinhardt by Optimo

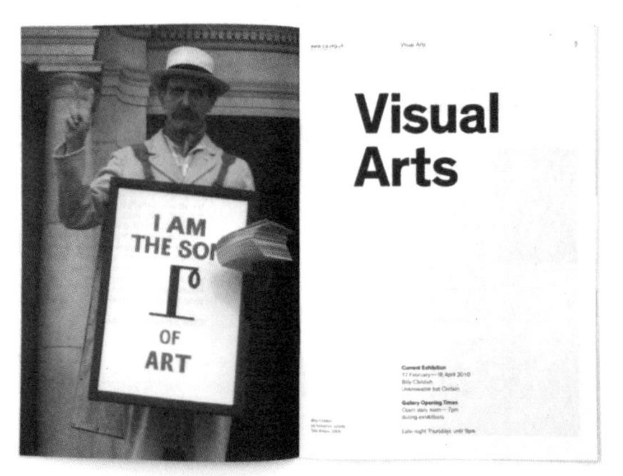

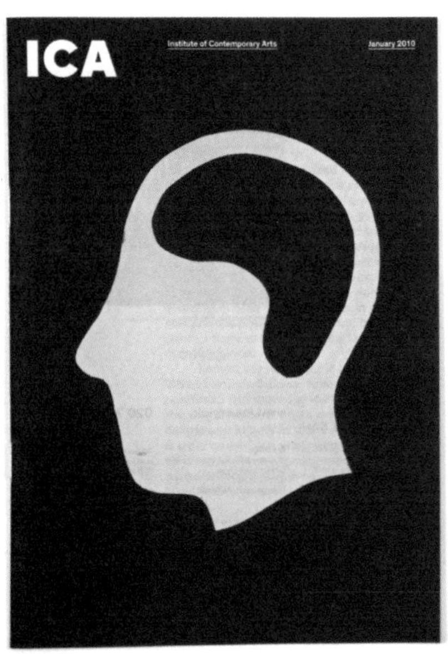

London
Inter-
national
Mime
Festival

For
the
blind
man
in
the
dark
room
looking
for
the
black
cat
that
isn't
there
3—23 December, 2—31 January
This acclaimed international group exhibition includes works by more than 20 modern and contemporary artists, including still lifes by Giorgio Morandi, a celebrated film by Fischli & Weiss, and a sculptural installation by Dave Hullfish Bailey.
The exhibition celebrates the speculative nature of knowledge, rejecting the common assumption that art is a code that needs cracking and presenting works that employ nonknowledge, unlearning and productive confusion as ways to understand the world.

Music

COSEY
COMPLEX
&
Cosey Club
Saturday 27 March
1—6pm (Complex)
10pm—3am (Club)
Artists'
Film Club
Haris
Epaminonda
Monday 22 March
7pm

Design **Client**

JULTA **20 HOXTON SQUARE , UK**

Title
The Embassy

Specifications
Size:
205mm x 255mm, 96 pages
Colour & Print:
CMYKoffset
Paper:
cover: Fedrigoni Constelation Snow, 250gsm
inner pages: Fedrigoni Splendorgel, 140gsm, Fedrigoni Vellum, 100gsm
Binding:
perfect bind

The Embassy was an exhibition that took place at the former Embassy of Sierra Leone in London where the building was used as diplomatic facilities of a fictional, problematic country. Use of understated typography for the catalogue gives it a bureaucratic feel, a deliberate reference to the official theme of the exhibition. This is also reflected in the cover, featuring the United Nations official blue passport paper.

THE VAGARIES
OF TIME TRAVEL
AND
THE PROBLEMS
WITH PASTICHE

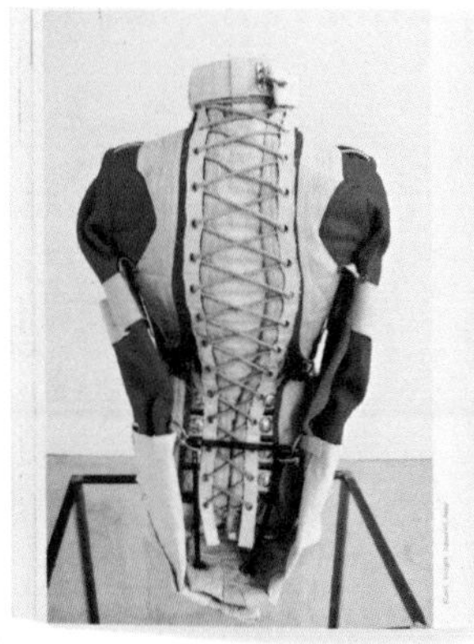

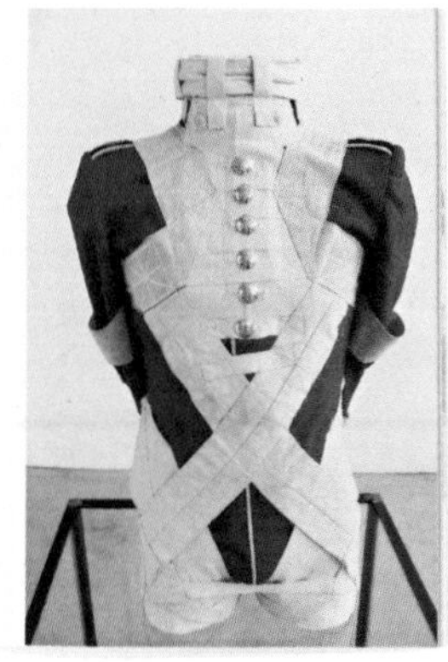

MARCEL BRUER,
LIVE AT THE HAGUE

WALLACE K. HARRISON SINGS WITH BUENA VISTA SOCIAL CLUB IN HAVANA

WALTER GROPIUS PRESENTS: BOUZOUKI SERENADES IN ATHENS

JOSE LUIS SERT DEBUTS HIS COMPOSITIONS FOR OUD IN BAGHDAD

RICHARD NEUTRA PERFORMS SURFIN' USA AND OTHER BEACH BOYS CLASSICS IN KARACHI

EERO SAARINEN SINGS HIS A CAPPELLA RENDITION OF ELVIS' BLUE SUEDE SHOES IN LONDON

CESAR PELLI PERFORMS ASTURIAS AND OTHER FLAMENCO GUITAR MASTERPIECES IN TOKYO

MARCEL BRUER COVERS ELVIS COSTELLO'S ALISON IN PARIS

CHRISTIAN DE POTZAMPARC: ERIK SATIE NOCTURNES IN BERLIN

EDWARD DURELL STONE PERFORMS AARON COPLAND'S OLD AMERICAN SONGS ON SOLO PIANO IN NEW DELHI

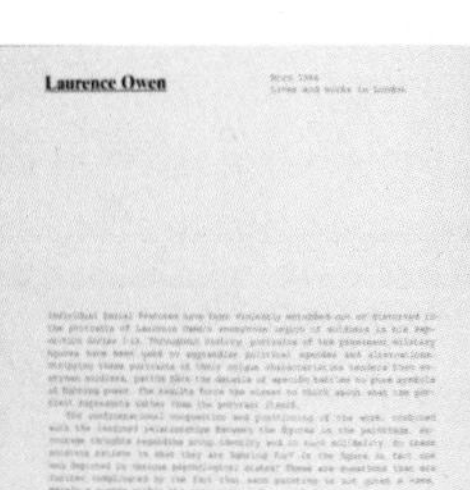

Laurence Owen

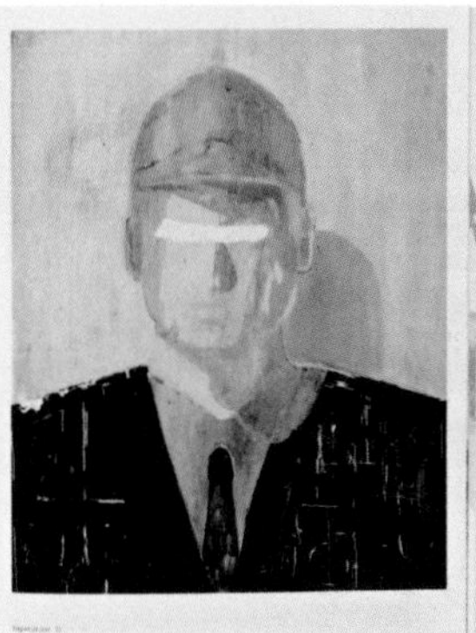

Design STUDIO BAER

Client BISCHOFF / WEISS GALLERY, UK

Title
Nathaniel Rackowe Artist Catalogue

Specifications
Size:
A5
Colour & Print:
4-colour, litho
Paper:
cover: pristine white coated paper
inner pages: white uncoated paper
Binding:
perfect bind
Finishing:
laser cut cover

Binding:

PERFECT BIND

:3

Chapter Three:

CHARITY & PUBLIC SECTOR

As with all the client sectors in this book, there is no set style when designing for charities. However, working for charities frequently involves larger type sizes for legibility and accessibility. The work by Wire Design provides some interesting examples of attractive design solutions using bigger type size and proves that accessible type doesn't need to be limiting. pp. 115, 132

In design, any work undertaken can become more meaningful when you share the message and passion of your client. It becomes even more rewarding when you see the real impact on people's lives that some charities can make, as well as how design can help them to convey their message and help reach people.

The work done by Studio EMMI for The Prince's Foundation for Children & the Arts is a prime personal example. The studio has designed a number of materials for the Children & the Arts almost from its inception, designing – to give just one example – the organisation's annual reports over several years. Building a relationship with this client over time has given the studio the opportunity to broaden and deepen their creative practice together. p. 136

Design	**Client**
WIRE | REFUGEE COUNCIL, UK

Title
Don't Believe the Type

Specifications
Colour:
envelope: 2-colours (Pantone)
Paper:
silk coated, 250gsm
Finishing:
envelope: die-cut stencil lettering
contents: T-shirt, stickers, booklet, badges and a return card

Design

FONS HICKMANN M23

Client

AMNESTY INTERNATIONAL, GERMANY

Title

Amnesty Aktion Magazine

Specifications

Size:
310mm x 470mm, 8 pages

Colour & Print:
4-colour, offset

Binding:
saddle stitch

This paper is distributed at demonstrations and political events. Each issue contains a spread that strikingly displays statistics, in most cases covering a specific topic. The magazine illustrates the international significance of certain processes with a call for action, inviting the readers to actively participate.

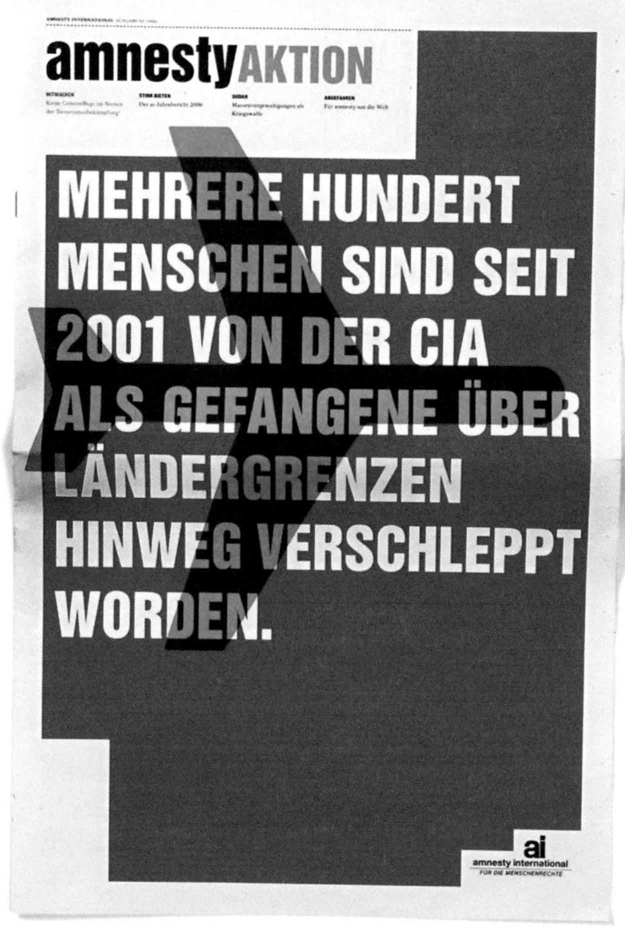

amnesty
ERFOLGE
Ihr Brief kann Leben retten
FRAUEN IN SAUDI-ARABIEN
MITMACHEN
Einsatz für Zeynab Beyazıdi

AMNESTY INTERNATIONAL
amnestyAKTION
MITMACHEN
Keine Folter in Ägypten!
TODESSTRAFE
Aktuelle Zahlen und Fakten
MUSIK
Musiker unterstützen amnesty international
ERFOLGE
Ihr Brief kann Leben retten

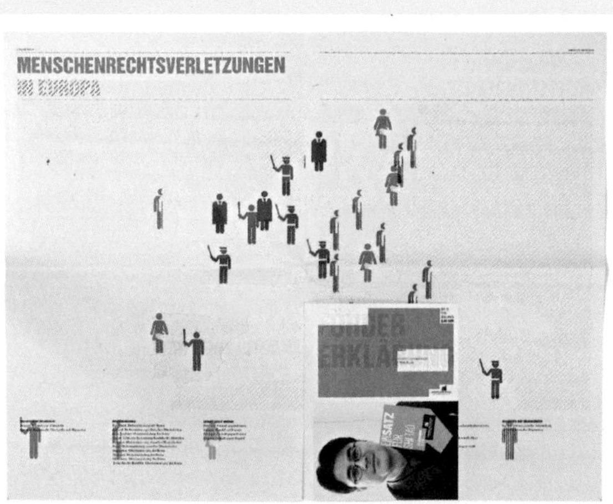
MENSCHENRECHTSVERLETZUNGEN
IN EUROPA

Design PENTAGRAM

Client SHELTER, UK

Title
House of Cards

Specifications

Size:
card slipcase: 217mm x 177mm
cards and invitation: A5
book: A4, 64 pages plus cover

Colour & Print:
cards: CMYK / 1-colour
invitation: 2-colour
book: CMYK

Paper:
card slipcase: GF Smith Colorplan Ebony over board
invitation: GF Smith Colorplan Ice White, 540gsm
book cover: Horizon Offset, 140gsm
book inner pages: Horizon Offset, 300gsm

Finishing:
rounded corners for the cards; invitation and book foil blocked

Shelter
In association with
invite you (plus guest) to the
launch party and private view of
The House of Cards Exhibition
Participating artists
Marc Quinn
Damien Hirst
Amelia's Magazine
Amanda Levete Architects
M/M (Paris)
Gillian Wearing
WN Studio
Rob Ryan
Boo Ritson
Miles Aldridge
Polly Morgan
Gerald Scarfe
Basso & Brooke
Dan Baldwin
Giles Deacon
Ron Arad
Paul Fryer
Sophie Conran
Rachel Whiteread
Nick Park
Kyle Cooper
Eine
Hew Locke
Sir Terence Conran
Jake & Dinos Chapman
Vivienne Westwood
Alexander McQueen
Tim Walker
Simon Henwood
Ella Doran
Henry Holland
Barbara Hulanicki
Neasden Control Centre
Rachel Howard
Julie Verhoeven
Experimental Jetset
Stephen Webster
Mat Collishaw
Tom Hunter
Rankin
Antoni & Allison
NB Studio
Rachel Thomas
Neville Brody
Lacey with Hana Al Sayed
Simon Patterson
Michael Craig Martin
Public competition winner
Jon Burgerman
Jamie Reid
Douglas Gordon
D*Face
David Bailey

Design

STUDIO EMMI

Client

THE PRINCE'S FOUNDATION FOR CHILDREN & THE ARTS, UK

Title

MusicQuest Book for Teachers

Specifications

Size:
210mm x 250mm, 48 pages plus 8-page short cover

Colour & Print:
2-colour (Pantone Cyan and Pantone 302), litho printed using vegetable-based inks

Paper:
cover: GF Smith Colorplan Pristine White, 270gsm, FSC certified, 100% ECF virgin fibre, acid free
inner pages: Beckett Expression Radiance, 118gsm, FSC certified, 100% ECF virgin fibre, made with wind energy

Binding:
loop stitch

The MusicQuest Book is bound with loop stitches so teachers can store it in a durable ring binder, together with variable A4 student sheets.

Illustrations: Emily Alston

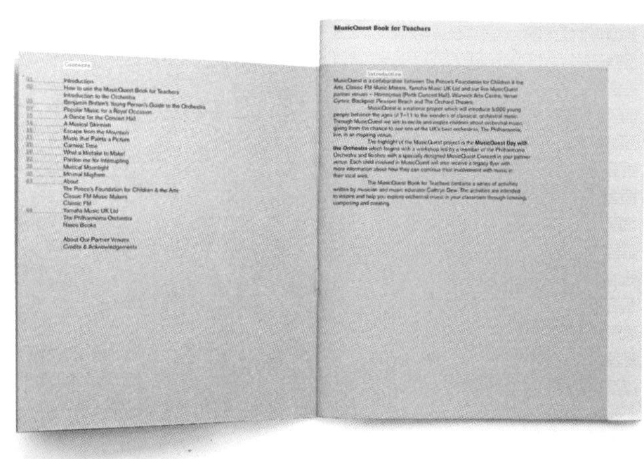

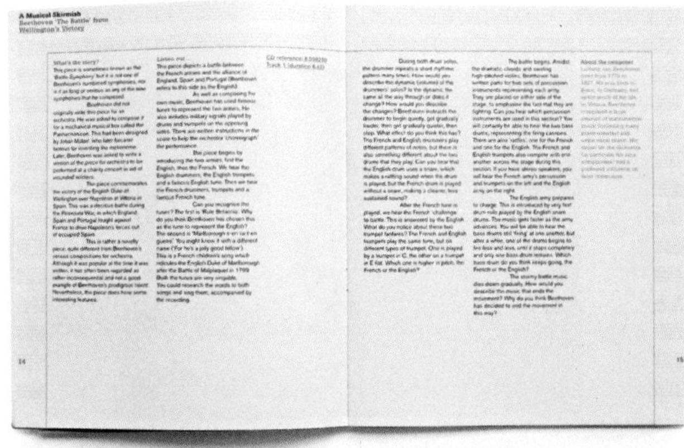

Binding:

LOOP STITCH

Design

WEBB & WEBB

Client

ROYAL SOCIETY OF ARTS, UK

Title
Drugs – Facing Facts
The Report of the RSA Commission on Illegal Drugs, Communities and Public Policy

Specifications
Size:
A4, 336 pages
Colour & Print:
text pages: 1-colour
section dividers: 2-colour, using vegetable-based inks
Paper:
recycled stock
Binding:
notched perfect bind

Appendix

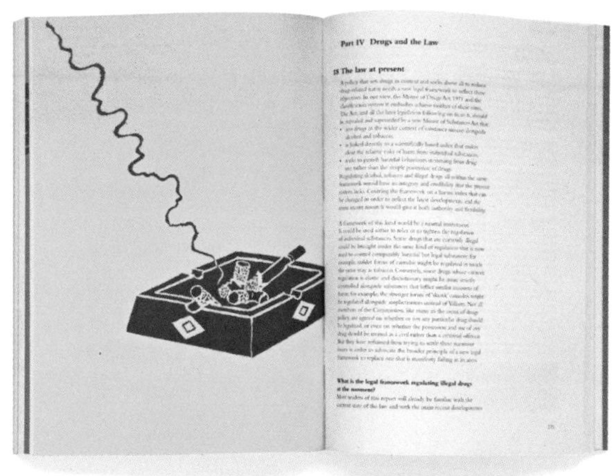
Part IV Drugs and the Law
15 The law at present

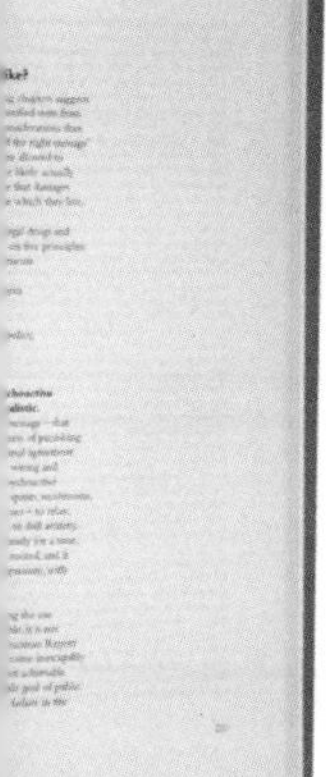

Part II Drugs policy at the moment
8 The evolution of drugs policy

Design	Client
ESPIRELTUS	**LUIS SIMARRO, SPAIN**

Title
Tarjeta de Navidad

Specifications
Size:
180mm x 155mm
Colour & Print:
CMYK
Paper:
paper made from chlorine-free pulp
Finishing:
die cut

Illustration by Sergio Montal

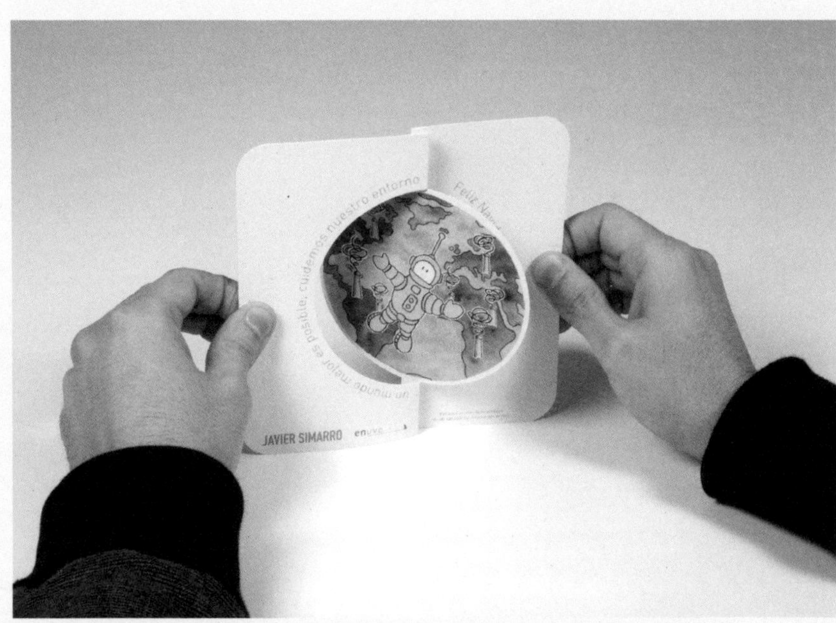

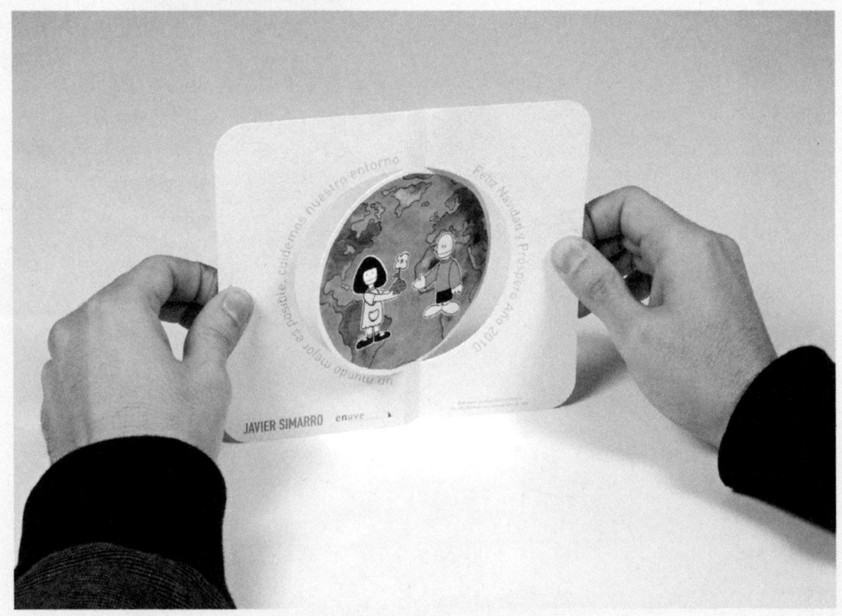

Design | Client

KENN MUNK | WWF (VERDENSNATURFONDEN, DENMARK)

Title
Save the Ice

Specifications
Size:
DIN A4
Colour & Print:
CMYK, by ISO14001 certified printer
Paper:
Trucard Gloss, 220gsm, FSC certified
Finishing:
die cut

Design

HEY

Client

OXFAM, SPAIN

Title
Intermón Oxfam

Specifications
Size:
A2
Colour:
1-colour (black)
Paper:
Pop'Set

DaleLaVueltaAlMundo.org
Intermón
Oxfam

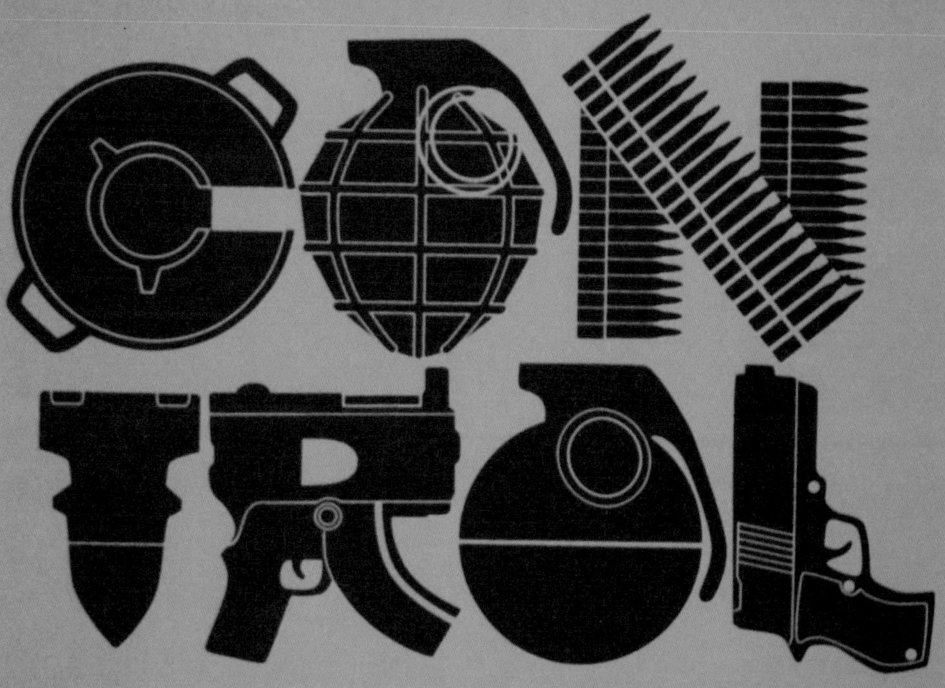
ARMAS BAJO
CONTROL

Design	**Client**
OPTIMASTUDIO	**OPTIMASTUDIO, SPAIN**

Title
Designs for All

Specifications
Size:
poster: 700mm x 1000mm
Colour & Print:
CMYK plus Pantone
Paper:
Munken Pure, 170gsm
Binding:
casebound book with headbands and tailbands; green ribbon bookmark bound into the book at the top of the spine
Finishing:
poster wrapped around the book and fixed with a bespoke cloth measuring tape

Binding:

HEADBAND AND TAILBAND

Diseño a la medida de todas las personas
Design tailored for everyone
Acercamientos Personales

Mira, escucha & aprende
Look, Listen & Learn
Diseños para Todos
Designs for All

Design | **Client**

COAST | **EURODAD, BELGIUM**

Title
Eurodad Fight Capital Fight campaign

Specifications
Size:
box: 220mm x 320mm
postcards: 20 A6 postcards
report 1: 180mm x 240mm
report 2: A4
Colour & Print:
CMYK plus 2-colour (Pantone metallic and bronze)
Paper:
a selection of Sappi papers
Finishing:
report 2: foil blocked cover

Eurodad is a network of 54 European NGOs working to change development finance policies and to ensure that poorer people influence decisions that affect their lives. Fight Capital Flight campaign informed decision makers about the multiple aspects of the north/south financial gap. The campaign included a fact box with a memorandum manifesto, facts postcards and three poverty/luxury posters.

NORTH
SOUTH
IMPACT OF FINANCIAL MARKETS ON DEVELOPING COUNTRIES

CAPITAL FLIGHT FACT:
DEVELOPING COUNTRIES
INFLOW $875 BILLION
OUTFLOW $1205 BILLION

NORTH
SOUTH

Invest in Africa!
Give 1 $
Get 5 $ back!
Playing financial roulette: Sub-Saharan Africa loses an average of $13 billion every year, this means $35.6 million per day.

GIVING
TAKING

Design | **Client**

WIRE | **EMPLOYER'S FORUM FOR DISABILITY, UK**

Title
Unravelling the Knot Invite

Specifications
Size:
A5
Colour:
1-colour
Paper:
GF Smith Colorplan, 350gsm
Folding:
A4 folded to A5
Finishing:
foil blocking

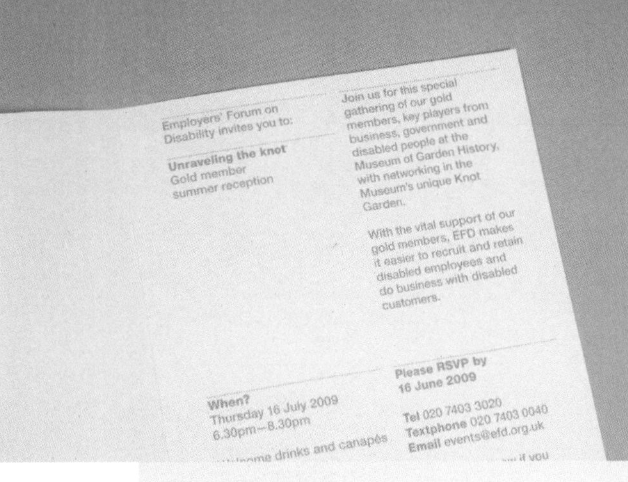

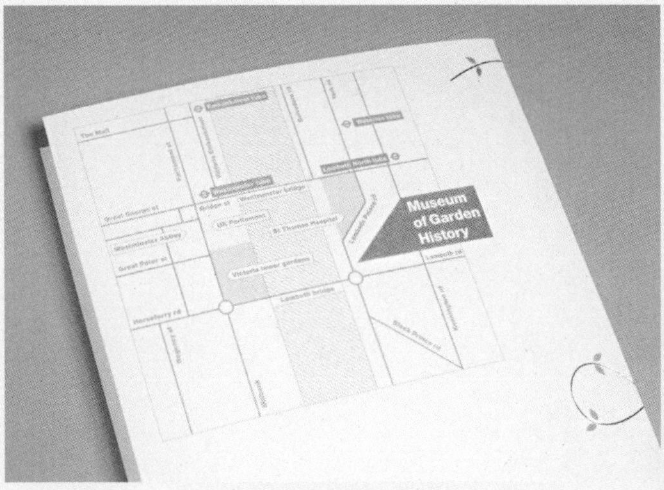

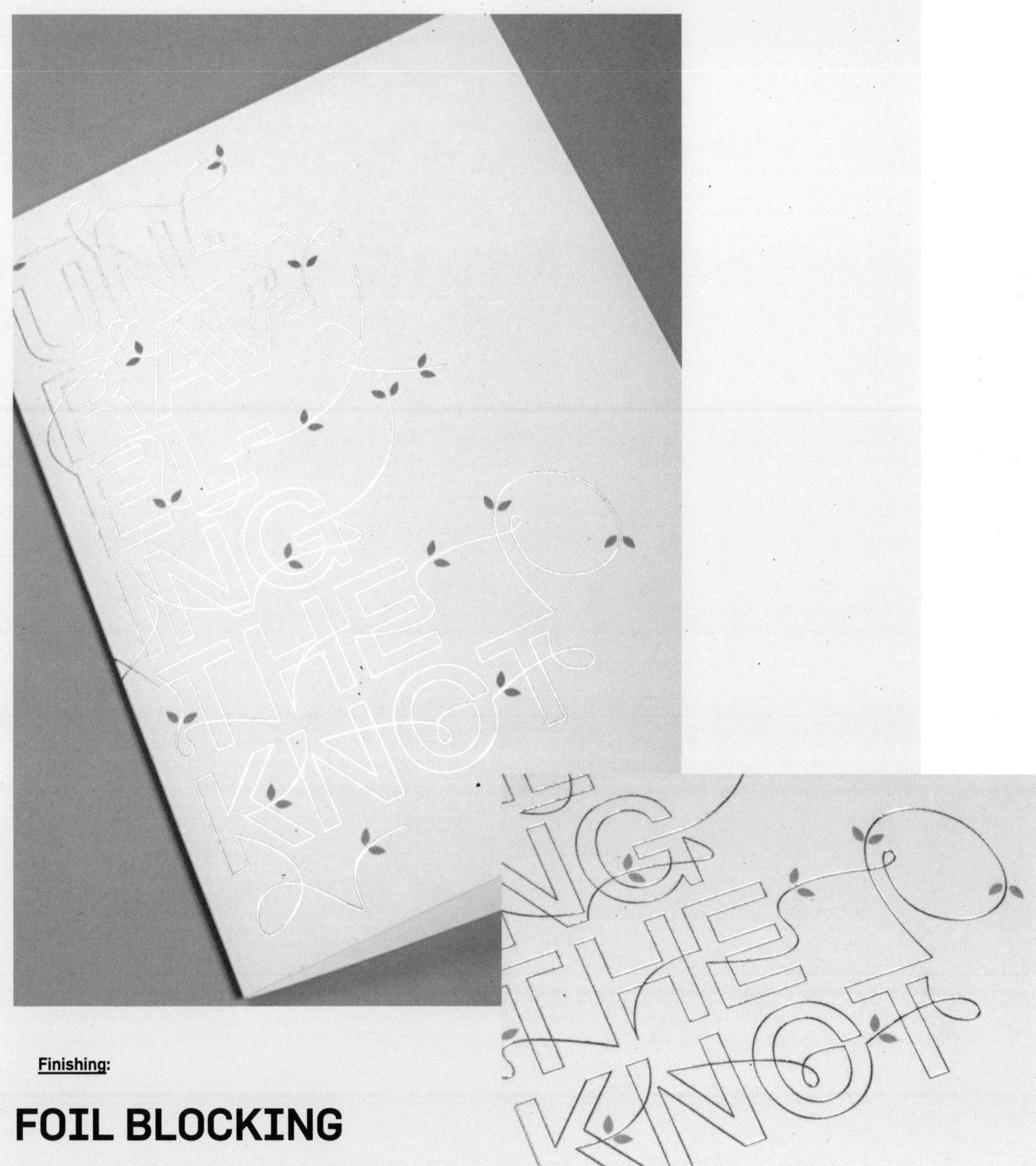

Finishing:

FOIL BLOCKING

Design | **Client**

MONIQUE KNEEPKENS | IN AFRICA FOUNDATION, AUSTRALIA

Title
Sustainable Christmas Card

Specifications
Size:
A5 card that folds out to A3 poster
Colour & Print:
CMYK
Paper:
100% recycled

As an example of a multi-purpose sustainable approach, the logo can be peeled off, turning the poster into Christmas wrapping paper.

SEASONS
GREETINGS
TO YOU ALL
BEST WISHE
S AND A WO
NDERFUL NE
W YEAR MAY
THERE BE
HOPE AND P
EACE OPPOR
TUNITY AND
PROSPERIT
Y AND JOY
IN AFRICA
© In Africa Foundation Ltd.

Design | **Client**

STUDIO EMMI | **THE PRINCE'S FOUNDATION FOR CHILDREN & THE ARTS, UK**

Title
Annual Reviews:
2006/7, 2007/8 and 2008/9

Specifications
Size:
A5, 32 pages
Colour & Print:
cover: 2-colour (Pantone Magenta and Pantone 229)
inner pages: CMYK, vegetable-based inks
Paper:
2006/7
cover: Gmund Bier Weizen
inner pages: Revive 50-50 Offset
2007/8
cover: Metaphor
inner pages: Context
2008/9
cover: Corona Offset, 300gsm
inner pages: Emerald Repro, 115gsm
Folding:
2008/9: back cover flap folded over fore-edge
Binding:
perfect bind

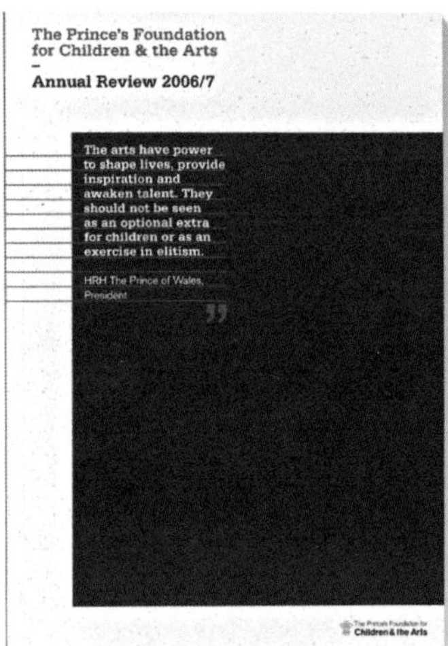

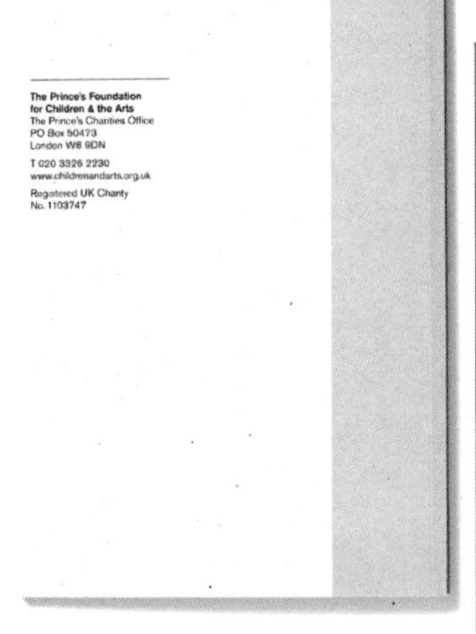

The Prince's Foundation
for Children & the Arts
The Prince's Charities Office
PO Box 50473
London W8 9DN
T 020 3326 2230
www.childrenandarts.org.uk
Registered UK Charity
No. 1103747

The Prince's Foundation
for Children & the Arts
Annual Review 2008/9
The rich traditions, stories and
magic of music, dance, theatre
and fine art really do need to
be easily available and accessible
to every child in our country.
HRH The Prince of Wales, President
Children & the Arts

Title
Renaissance: The Revitalisation of Elephant & Castle

Specifications

Colour:
inner pages: 5-colour

Paper:
dust jacket: GF Smith Colorplan
cover: GF Smith Colorplan
inner pages: Satin, 150gsm

Finishing:
UV varnish on inner pages; embossing and 2-colour foil blocking on dust jacket

Renaissance:
The revitalisation
of Elephant & Castle

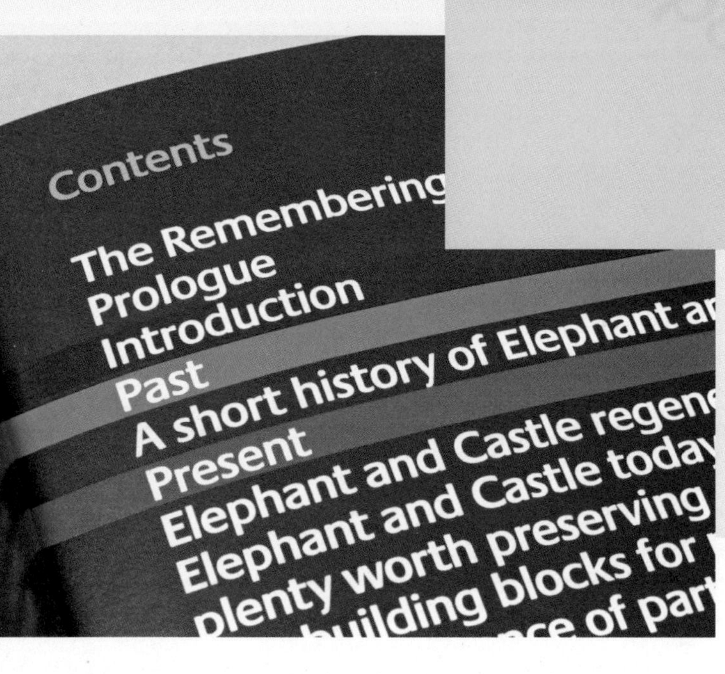
Contents
The Remembering
Prologue
Introduction
Past
A short history of Elephant
Present
Elephant and Castle
Elephant and Castle
plenty worth preserving
building blocks for

Design | **Client**

LUCIENNE ROBERTS + | **PANOS LONDON, UK**

Title
Growing Pains: How Poverty and AIDS Are Challenging Childhood

Specifications
Size:
210mm x 160mm
Colour & Print:
cover: 1-colour, silkscreen
pages 1-216: 1-colour
pages 217-236: CMYK
pages 237-252: 1-colour
Paper:
cover: 2mm strawboard
pages 1-216: Cyclus offset, 100gsm
pages 217-236: Cyclus offset, 140gsm
pages 237-252: Cyclus offset, 100gsm
Binding:
section sewn with coloured cloth spine and affixed front and back covers

Design: Lucienne Roberts/
John McGill

This engaging book, commissioned by the Bernard van Leer Foundation, brings new perspectives to the debate about AIDS by relating the experiences of young children in South Africa, as well as some instances in Tanzania and Kenya. First-hand accounts of children, caregivers and community workers illuminate efforts to bridge the gulf between policies based on children's rights and the experience of millions of young children.

Anthony Swift and Stan Maher's in-depth and candid accounts of grassroots interventions emphasise the importance of early childhood development. They draw attention to basic needs that are often unmet amid the endemic challenges of sickness, poverty and stigma.

The authors explore the mutual support provided by children, families, community members and local organisations and argue that this local reciprocity is increasingly under threat.

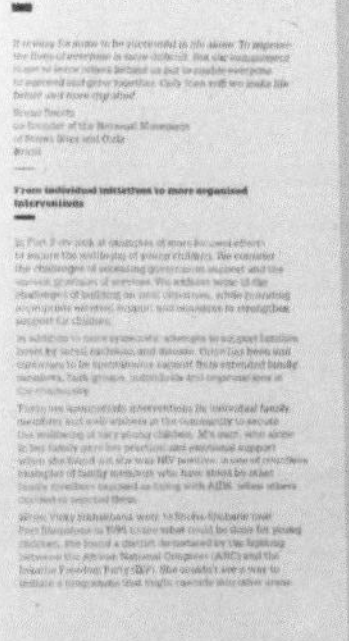

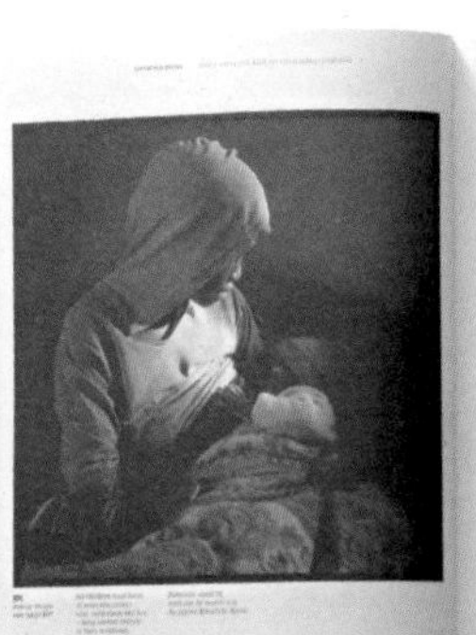

Design
B&W STUDIO

Client
SHOWING EXPECTATIONS, UK

Title
Showing Expectations

Specifications
Size:
155mm x 215mm
Colour:
1-colour (black)
Paper:
cover: Dutch greyboard, 300gsm, EFC certified
dustjacket and inner pages: Pop'Set, 120gsm

A visual arts project titled 'Showing: Expectations' invited six Leeds-based community groups, which are identified on educational and organisational databases as being under-represented in higher education and the creative sectors, to participate in and curate their own art exhibition. The community groups involved were: Workers' Educational Association, St Anne's Resource Centre & Open Learning, Gypsy Roma Traveller Achievement Service Leeds, Emmaus – Leeds Community, South Leeds Health for All Asian Elders and St George's Crypt.

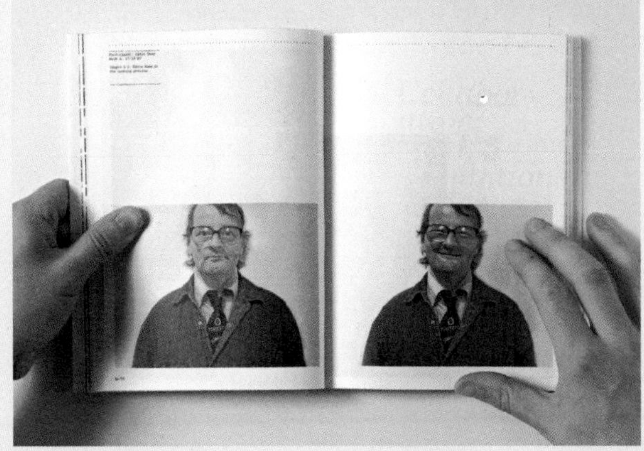

Format:

DUST JACKET

Design	Client
TANGENT GRAPHIC	SCOTTISH HUMAN RIGHTS COMMISSION, UK

Title
Annual Report

Specifications
Size:
A4, 36 pages
Colour & Print:
CMYK
Paper:
Revive Pure White 100%, recycled stock
Binding:
saddle stitch
Finishing:
laser cut cover

Design | **Client**

B&W STUDIO | **ST GEORGE'S CRYPT, UK**

Title
Annual Report and 6 Accounts

Specifications

Size:
A2, 24 pages

Colour & Print:
CMYK

Paper:
Arctic Volume White, 100gsm, FSC certified

Folding:
A2 folds to A3

Binding:
self-cover, loose-leaf document

Finishing:
sent out in polybag

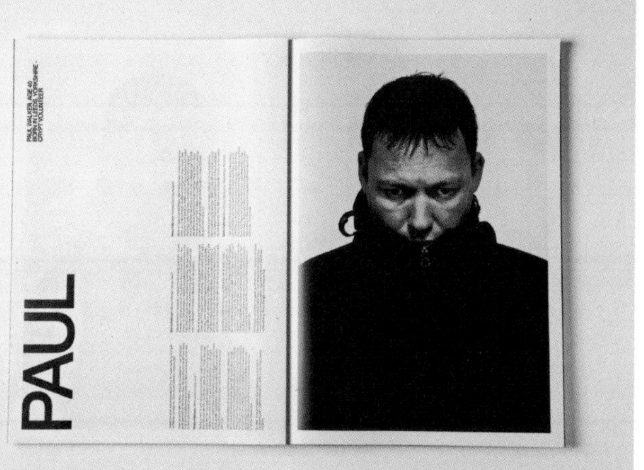

Design | **Client**

STUDIO EMMI | **THE PRINCE'S FOUNDATION FOR CHILDREN & THE ARTS, UK**

Title
Catalyst

Specifications
Size:
A4, 124 pages
Colour & Print:
CMYK, vegetable-based inks
Paper:
cover: Munken Print White, FSC certified
inner pages: Arctic Volume White, FSC certified
Binding:
perfect bind
Finishing:
Includes a bookmark with a fold

Illustrations by Lucy Vigrass

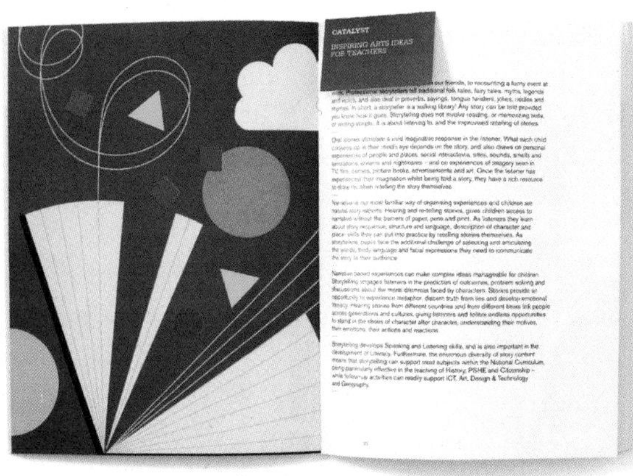

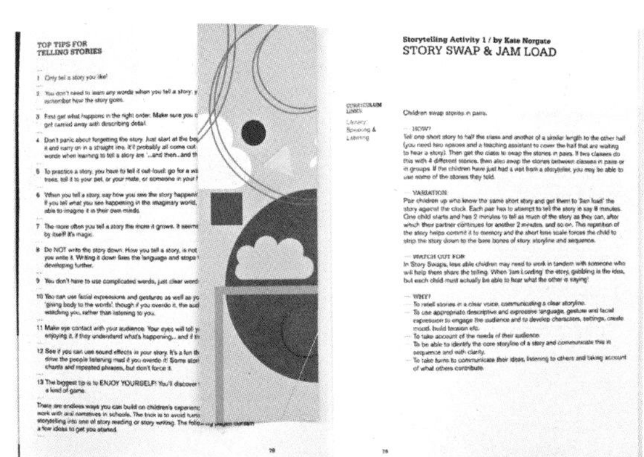

:4

Chapter Four:

CULTURE

The designs showcased in this chapter are made for a wide client list, and bears the title 'Culture' as a catch-all for those inspiring projects that are not otherwise easily catalogued.

Case studies such as the posters and flyers designed by Julia for Invisible Dot, a London-based comedy production company, include some exemplary cost effective design solutions. Invisible Dot constantly needs documents to be made quickly at a low cost and quantity. Julia's solution was to use Risograph printers and design a distinctive typeface, Riso, which would establish the identity while also answering the brief beyond the client's expectations. p. 172

Another example of a resource saving, environmentally friendly design solution is by This Is Real Art for the International Society of Typographic Designers' *Typographic* 65 magazine. Titled 'The Advertising Issue', it persuaded the designer Paul Belford to print the majority of the magazine onto distinctive blue backs of randomly trimmed, unused advertising posters, paper that otherwise would have been pulped. This created a series of random alternate spreads throughout the magazine, making each magazine unique. p. 170

Design

Client

STUDIO EMMI

THE FINNISH INSTITUTE IN LONDON, UK

Title
(p)review

Specifications
Size:
A5, 32 pages
Colour & Print:
cover: short cover, flush at foot only, no print
front and back section: 2-colour (Pantone)
middle section: CMYK, vegetable-based inks
Paper:
cover: Keaykolour Antique Seal
front and back section: Keaykolour Recycled May
middle section: Chromomat
Binding:
saddle stitch
Finishing:
die cut slots for business card

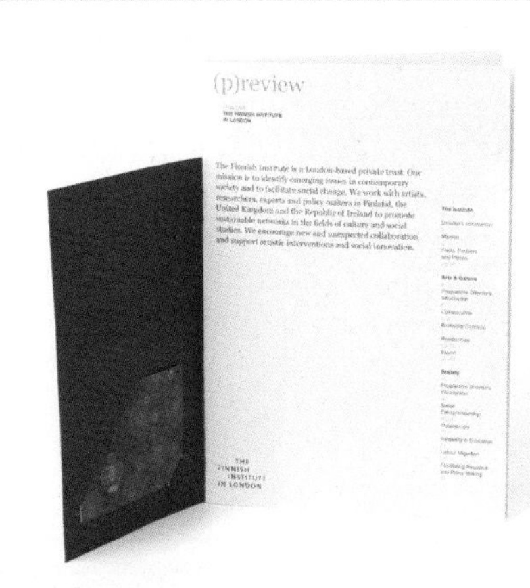

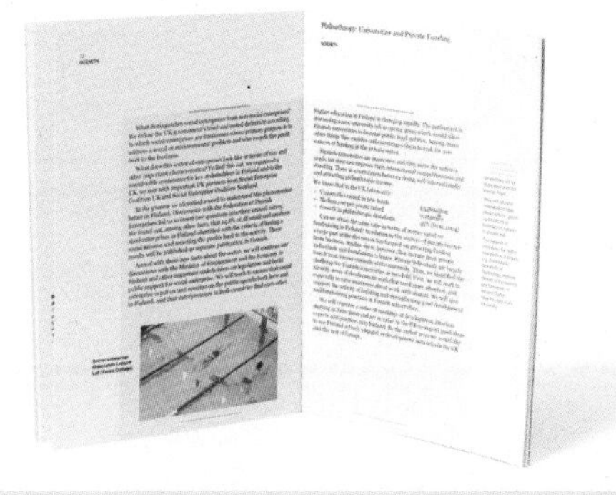

Finishing:

DIE CUT

Design | **Client**

FORM | **ARTS & BUSINESS, UK**

Title
29th Arts & Business Awards Brochure

Specifications
Size:
170mm x 255mm, 32 pages
Paper:
Plike
Binding:
saddle stitch
Finishing:
high-gloss laminate finishes and foil blocking; the cover features a wraparound flap with silver and white foil blocking; the back of the flap has perforated swatches that were torn off for voting slips

Arts & Business aspires to be the world's most successful & widespread creative network. We help business people support the arts & the arts inspire business people, because good business & great art together create a richer society.

Celebrating a future built on ideas and creativity

Baroness Helena Kennedy QC
Chair

Colin Tweedy
Chief Executive

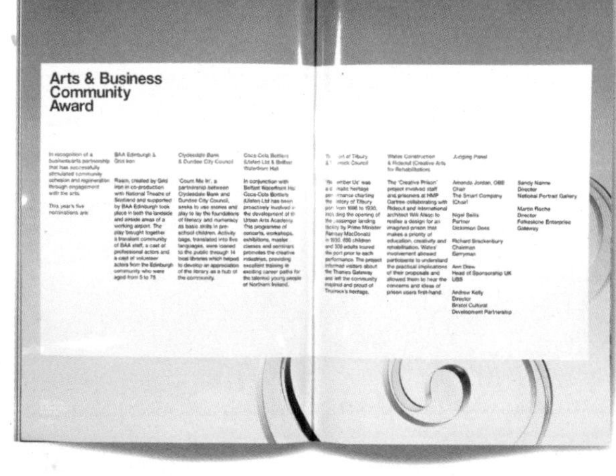

Design | **Client**

WORLDSTUDIO | **THE FASHION CENTER BUSINESS IMPROVEMENT DISTRICT, USA**

Title
A Stitch in Time: A History of New York's Fashion District

Specifications
Size:
7" x 10", 28 pages plus cover
Colour:
3-colour (Black, PMS Yellow and PMS 424U)
Paper:
Mohawk Navajo Brilliant
Binding:
singer sewn through
Finishing:
coating throughout

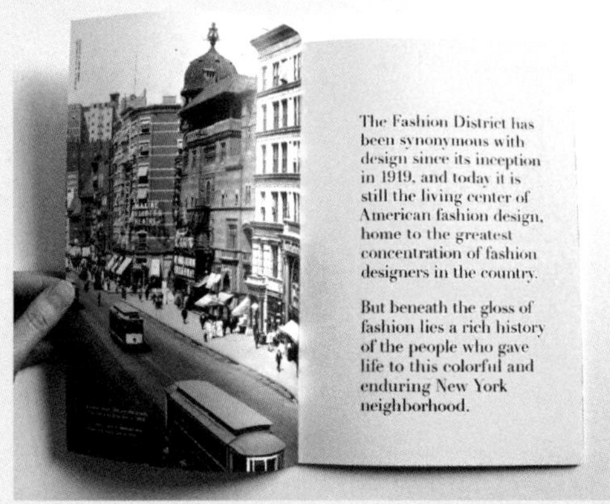

Binding:

SINGER SEWN THROUGH

Design

Client

VIA GRAFIK

HESSISCHES LANDESTHEATER MARBURG, GERMANY

Title
Inthega Brochure

Specifications
Size:
210mm x 210mm, 36 pages
Colour & Print:
CMYK, offset
Paper:
offset paper, 110gsm
Binding:
saddle stitch

Photos by Margaritha Brenner-Grigorowa

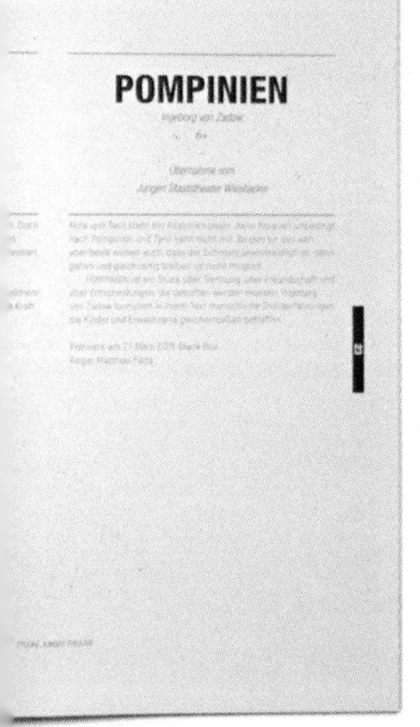

Design	Client
JORGE LORENZO	CONSEJERÍA DE CULTURA DEL PRINCIPADO DE ASTURIAS, SPAIN

Title
XX Muestra de Artes del Principado de Asturias

Specifications
Size:
A5, 128 pages
Colour & Print:
CMYK and duotone
Paper:
Plaster Velvet 2000 Vol Creator
Binding:
perfect bind
Finishing:
dust jacket

Print:

DUOTONE

Design

UNFOLDED

Client

THEATER DER KÜNSTE, ZÜRICH, SWITZERLAND

Title

Personen, Profile, Perspektiven

Specifications

Size:

148mm x 210mm

poster, flat: 564mm x 840mm

poster, folded: 150mm x 210mm

Colour & Print:

1/4, offset

Paper:

Chromolux 700, 180gsm / 90gsm

poster: z-pharma, 50gsm

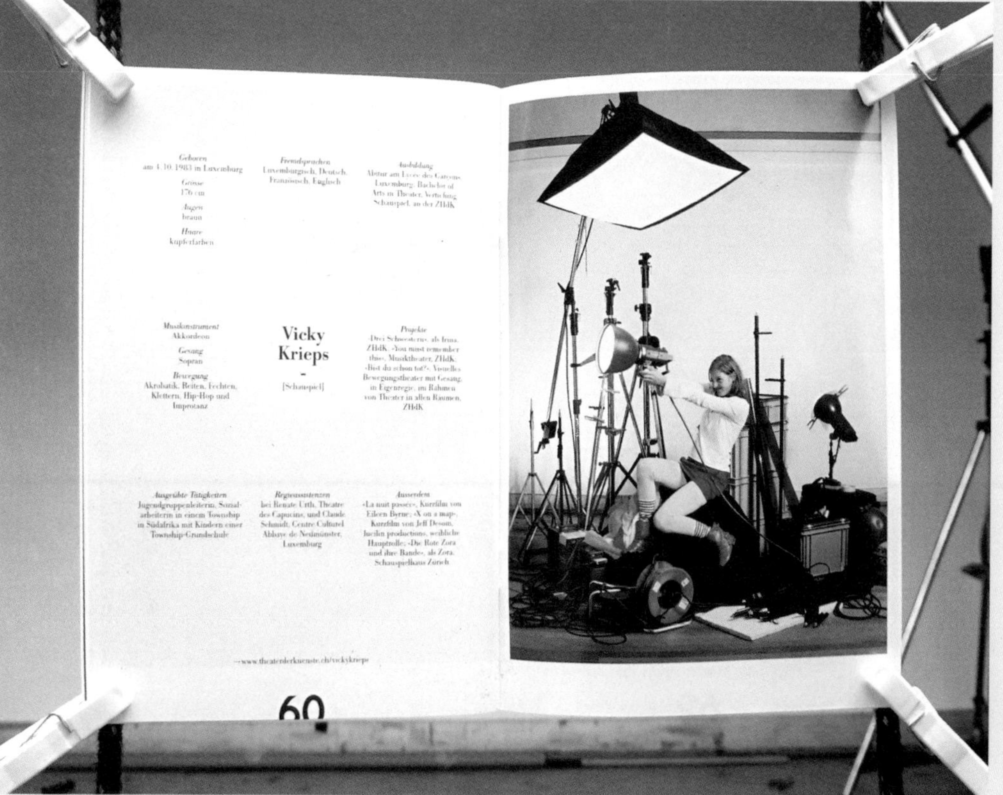

Geboren
am 4.10.1983 in Luxemburg
Grösse
176 cm
Augen
braun
Haare
kupferfarben
Fremdsprachen
Luxemburgisch, Deutsch, Französisch, Englisch
Ausbildung
Abitur am Lycée des Garçons Luxemburg, Bachelor of Arts in Theater, Vertiefung Schauspiel, an der ZHdK
Musikinstrument
Akkordeon
Gesang
Sopran
Bewegung
Akrobatik, Reiten, Fechten, Klettern, Hip-Hop und Improtanz
Vicky Krieps
-
[Schauspiel]
Projekte
«Drei Schwestern», als Irina, ZHdK; «You must remember this», Musiktheater, ZHdK; «Bist du schon tot?», Visuelles Bewegungstheater mit Gesang, in Eigenregie, im Rahmen von Theater in allen Räumen, ZHdK
Ausgeübte Tätigkeiten
Jugendgruppenleiterin, Sozialarbeiterin in einem Township in Südafrika mit Kindern einer Township-Grundschule
Regieassistenzen
bei Renate Urth, Theatre des Capucins, und Claude Schmidt, Centre Culturel Abbaye de Neumünster, Luxemburg
Ausserdem
«La nuit passée», Kurzfilm von Eileen Byrne; «X on a map», Kurzfilm von Jeff Desom, lucilin productions, weibliche Hauptrolle; «Die Rote Zora und ihre Bande», als Zora, Schauspielhaus Zürich
→www.theaterderkuenste.ch/vickykrieps
60

7
9
11
13
15
17
19
21
23
25
27
29
31
33
36
38
40
42
44
46
48
50
52
54
56
58
60
62

Charlotte Alten
-
[Schauspiel]
19

Design UNFOLDED

Client THEATER DER KÜNSTE, ZÜRICH, SWITZERLAND

Title
Masterplaner

Specifications
Size:
flat: 594mm x 420mm
folded: 148mm x 210mm
booklet insert: 105mm x 148mm
Colour & Print:
CMYK plus 1-colour (black), offset
Paper:
Munken Print Cream, 90gsm
Muskat Brown Paper, 100gsm
Econocolor Pink, 65gsm
Luxart gloss, 100gsm
Binding:
saddle stitch with red wire

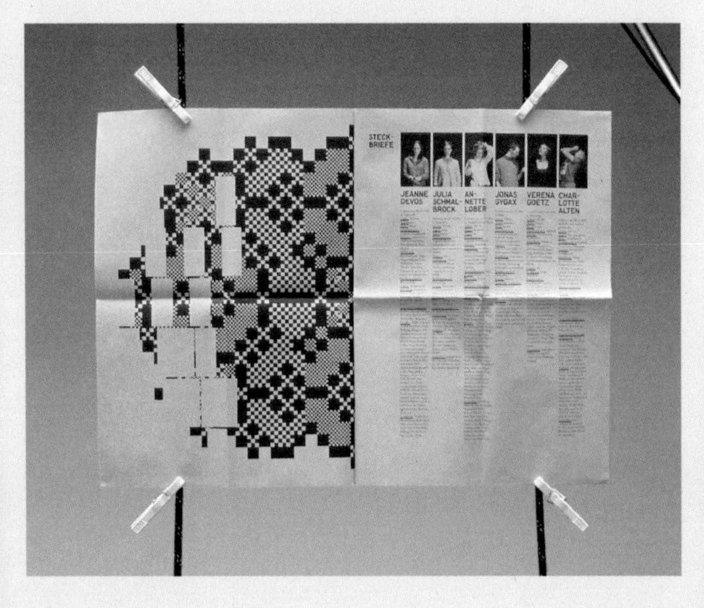
STECK-
BRIEFE
JEANNE
DEVOS
JULIA
SCHMAL-
BROCK
AN-
NETTE
LOBER
JONAS
GYGAX
VERENA
GOETZ
CHAR-
LOTTE
ALTEN

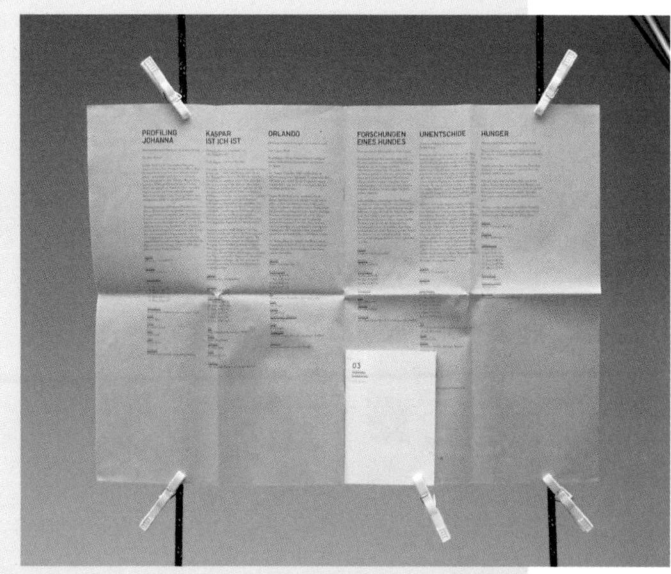
PROFILING
JOHANNA
KASPAR
IST ICH IST
ORLANDO
FORSCHUNGEN
EINES HUNDES
UNENTSCHIEDE
HUNGER
03

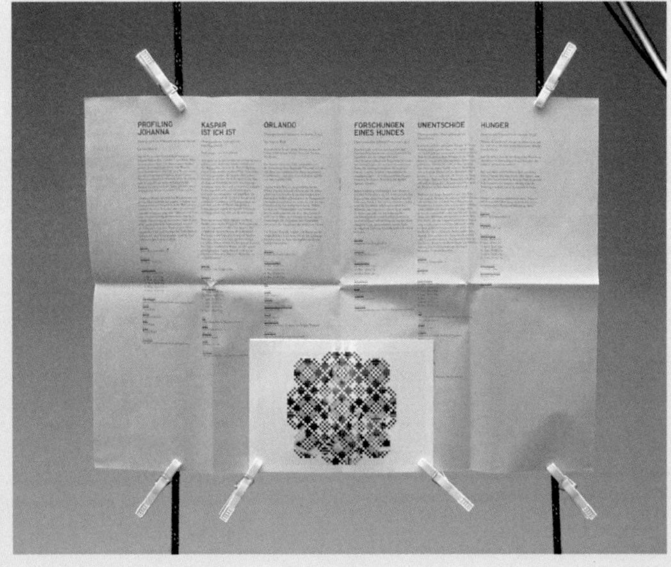
PROFILING
JOHANNA
KASPAR
IST ICH IST
ORLANDO
FORSCHUNGEN
EINES HUNDES
UNENTSCHIEDE
HUNGER

Design	Client
MARKO JOVANOVAC	OSJECKO LJETO KULTURE, CROATIA

Title
Završnica / Endgame

Specifications
Size:
flat: 630mm x 420mm
folded: 330mm x 145mm
Colour:
2-colour (black and red)
Paper:
Vega, 90gsm
Folding:
manually folded six times

ZAVRŠNICA
Samuel
Barclay
Beckett
(Endgame, 1958,
prema Fin de partie, 1957.)

Design

PAU LAMUÀ

Client

TEATRE PRINCIPAL D'OLOT, SPAIN

Title
Teatre Principal d'Olot

Specifications
Size:
leaflet: A3 folded to A6
programme: A6, 60 pages
Colour & Print:
2-colour
Paper:
Antalis Popset, different colours

TEATRE
PRINCIPAL
D'OLOT
SET.
OCT.
NOV.
DES.
2009

Design

FRASER MUGGERIDGE STUDIO

Client

CRAFTS COUNCIL, UK

Title

Collect Leaflets

Specifications

Size:
8-page leaflet

Colour & Print:
CMYK plus 2-colour

Paper:
coated and matt

Folding:
the first panel falls short, enabling the two different sides of the paper to be combined on the front of the leaflet

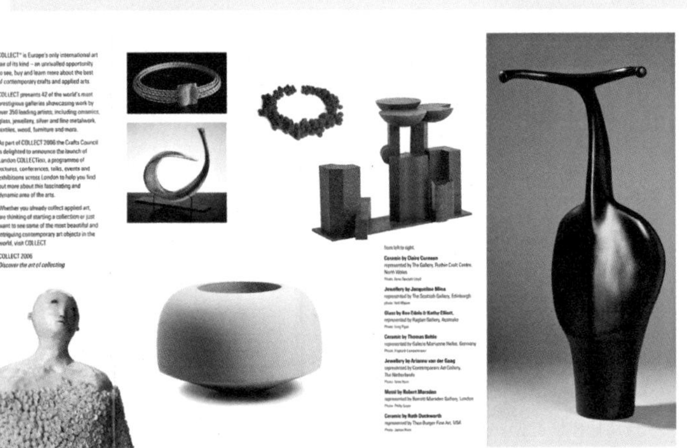

Design **Client**

EN PUBLIQUE **PROJECTBUREAU BELVEDERE, THE NETHERLANDS**

Title
Radio Kootwijk Frequency

Specifications
Size:
240mm x 170mm, 64 pages
Colour & Print:
3-colour (black, grey PMS and metallic PMS)
Paper:
cover: Hello silk, 350gsm
inner pages: Hello silk, 150gsm
Folding:
double folded cover
Binding:
sewn sections

Design

NIVARD THOES

Client

STICHTING NACHTWERK, THE NETHERLANDS

Title
DREBBEL

Specifications
Size:
216mm x 171mm, 112 pages
Colour & Print:
2-colour (PMS Black and PMS 485c), offset
Paper:
Pioneer 'Wood-Free' Offset, 110gsm
Cyclus Recycled Offset Paper, 80gsm
Binding:
sewn sections with open-spine stitch
Finishing:
hand-stamped imprints and handmade felt bookcasing

Finishing:

RUBBER STAMP

Design	Client
B&W STUDIO	LEEDS YOUTH OPERA, UK

Title
Der Freischutz Flyer

Specifications
Size:
210mm x 148mm, landscape
Colour:
1-colour (black)
Paper:
GF Smith Colorplan, Gmund Bier, Plike, Nomad (Omar), Heartland, 350gsm
Finishing:
shot by a hi-powered rifle from distance

Leeds Youth Opera
Presents
Der Freischütz
By Carl Maria von Weber
Der Freischütz

Design **Client**

THIS IS REAL ART **INTERNATIONAL SOCIETY OF TYPOGRAPHIC DESIGNERS, UK**

Title
Typographic 65
The Advertising Issue

Specifications
Size:
297mm x 210mm, 92 pages
Colour & Print:
CMYK
Paper:
printed mostly on blue backs of randomly trimmed, unused advertising posters, making each magazine unique
Binding:
thread-sewn section with dust jacket

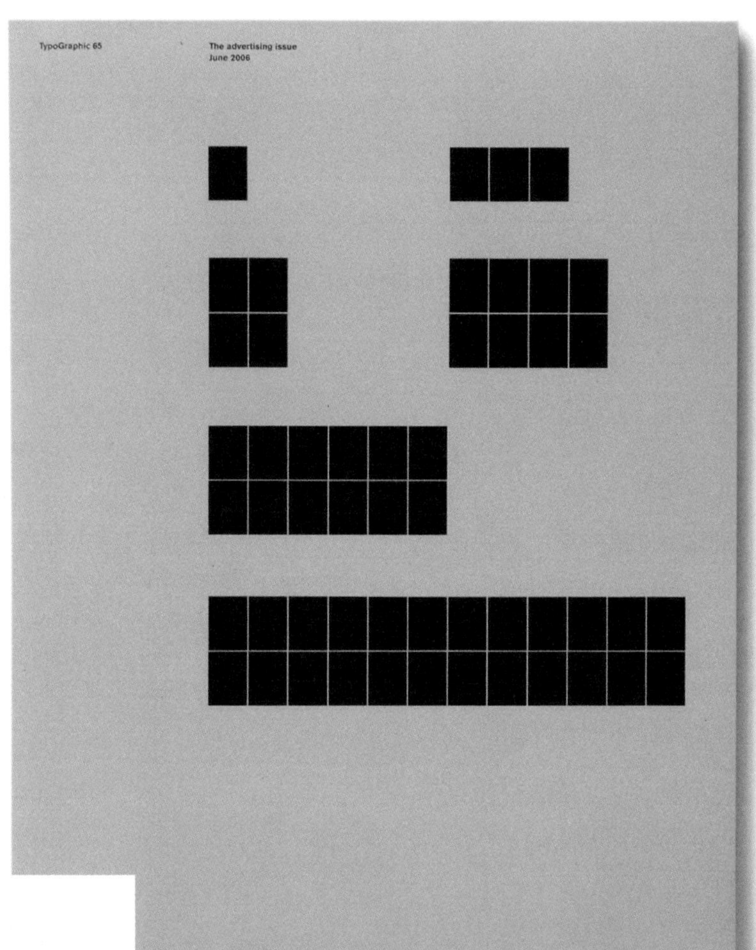

IBM
BAZAAR
Spring Fever
65 Pages of
Fashion Excitement
Paris
and America
Women Men Dote On
And Why

Letters
to the editor
if it
Takes
time -
Give it
Time

Design	Client
JULIA	THE INVISIBLE DOT, UK

Title
The Invisible Dot

Specifications
Size:
varied
Colour & Print:
1-colour and 2-colour, risograph
Paper:
various

The Invisible Dot, a comedy production company and venue in London, needed posters and flyers to be made quickly at low cost and quantities. The solution was to use Risograph printers and create a distinctive typeface that would establish the identity. The resulting type, Riso, has alternative characters with different widths to help the composition.

AABCDEEFFGGHHII
JKLMMNOPPQQRR
SSTUUVVWWXYZZ
0123456789 !#%&'()
*+,-./:;<>?@\`«´»£^¯"<>

The Invisible Dot.

Wednesday
08.09.09
8pm

The Invisible Dot
Camden Stables
Chalk Farm Road
NW1 8AH

For further information
0207 424 8918
info@theinvisibledot.com
www.theinvisibledot.com

£6

DANIEL
KITSON
WE ARE
GATHERED
HERE

The Invisible Dot.

Wednesday
22.09.09
8pm

The Invisible Dot
Camden Stables
Chalk Farm Road
NW1 8AH

For further information
020 7424 8918
info@theinvisibledot.com
www.theinvisibledot.com

£6

GHOST
GHOST
GHOST
GHOST
WATCH

The Invisible Dot.

Thursday
25.06.09
7pm

The Invisible Dot
Camden Stables
Chalk Farm Road
NW1 8AH

For further information
0207 424 8918
info@theinvisibledot.com
www.theinvisibledot.com

£6

JON
RICHARDSON
DAN
ATKINSON
LLOYD
LANGFORD
THE DOT
FARM

The Invisible Dot.

Wednesday
29.09.09
8pm

The Invisible Dot
Camden Stables
Chalk Farm Road
NW1 8AH

For further information
020 7424 8918
info@theinvisibledot.com
www.theinvisibledot.com

£6

ZELIG
ZE
ZELIG
ZELIG
ZE
WOODY ALLEN

The Invisible Dot.

Wednesday
15.09.09
8pm

The Invisible Dot
Camden Stables
Chalk Farm Road
NW1 8AH

For further information
020 7424 8918
info@theinvisibledot.com
www.theinvisibledot.com

£6

THE
FALLS

PETER
GREENAWAY

Design | **Client**

B&W STUDIO | **LEEDS YOUTH OPERA, UK**

Title
Idomeneo Programme

Specifications
Size:
poster: 470mm x 670mm
book: 168mm x 224mm, 32 pages, self-cover
Colour:
1-colour (black)
Paper:
poster: Chromolux White Label, 120gsm
book: Colorit Kingfisher Blue, 120gsm
Folding:
poster wraps around the book as dust jacket
Binding:
saddle stitch

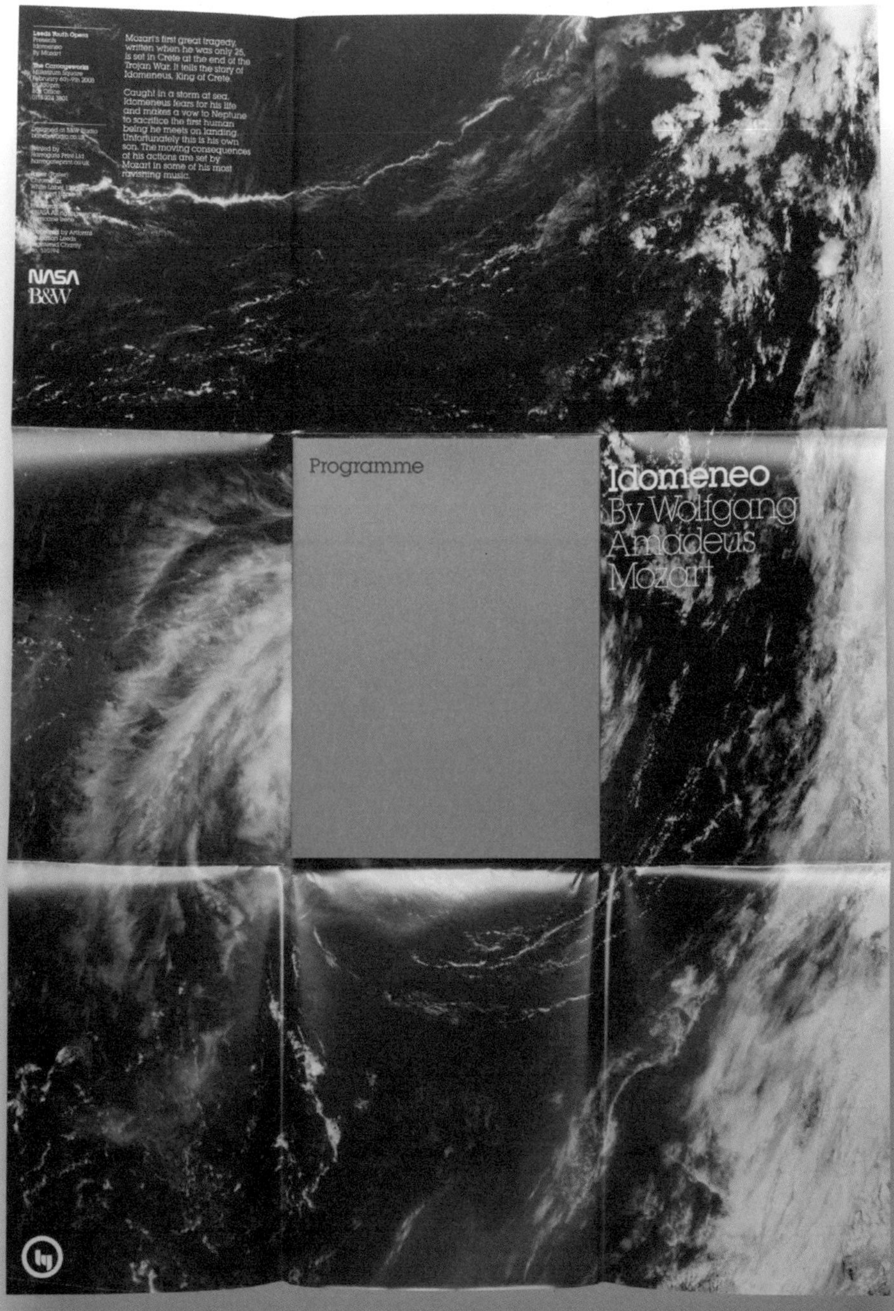
Leeds Youth Opera
Presents
Idomeneo
By Mozart
Mozart's first great tragedy, written when he was only 25, is set in Crete at the end of the Trojan War. It tells the story of Idomeneus, King of Crete.
Caught in a storm at sea, Idomeneus fears for his life and makes a vow to Neptune to sacrifice the first human being he meets on landing. Unfortunately this is his own son. The moving consequences of his actions are set by Mozart in some of his most ravishing music.
NASA
B&W
Programme
Idomeneo
By Wolfgang
Amadeus
Mozart

Design | **Client**

B&W STUDIO | **ROYAL INSTITUTE OF BRITISH ARCHITECTS, UK**

Title
RIBA Architects Awards

Specifications
Size:
images: A5, 8 pages
text: A6, 16 pages
Colour & Print:
CMYK plus fluorescent pink spot colour
Paper:
Arctic Volume Matt, 100gsm
Binding:
smaller brochure slides into the reverse of the larger brochure

WHITE
R
A
2

RIBA Yorkshire
Team 2009

RIBA Yorkshire region covers Yorkshire and the Humber and is directed by a Council elected from amongst its architect members. There are just over 2000 members in the region, which is divided into nine local branches.

The RIBA regions fulfil a vital co-ordinating role between RIBA members and the public. We provide core services for members and administer key RIBA strategies. We promote architecture and RIBA architect members through events and initiatives such as the awards schemes, CPD, regeneration debates, seminars, networking events and exhibitions.

Our office is based on The Calls, in the heart of Leeds design quarter and we share a beautifully converted Victorian riverside warehouse with built environment partners, architect practices and chartered surveyors.

Regional Team
(From left to right)

Geoff Ward
Regional Chair

Emma England
Regional Director

Claire Hutchinson
Marketing and Events Officer

Denise O'Toole
Membership and
Branch Liaison Officer

Regional Executive

David Smith
Vice Chair

John Orrell
Regional Treasurer

Robin Parker
Regional Secretary

Ian Collins
National Councillor

Gerard Bareham
National Councillor

Design	**Client**
GUDBERG	**RICKMERS, GERMANY**

Title
175 Years Rickmers

Specifications
Size:
folder: A4
booklet: A5, 36 pages
Colour:
2-colour (Pantone 876 U and Black)
Paper:
cover: Gmund Colors Subtil 50, 310 gsm, FSC certified, Gmund ECO certified
inner: Gmund Colors 50, 135gsm, FSC certified, Gmund ECO certified
Binding:
booklet: saddle stich
Finishing:
Paperlux™ paper etching

Binding:

PAPERLUX™ PAPER ETCHING

175 YEARS RICKMERS
The global crisis and roads to recovery
SYMPOSIUM-BOOKLET
175 YEARS RICKMERS

Design

Client

DÚOTIL

UNIÓN DE ABOGADOS EUROPEOS, SPAIN

Title
Publicación cultural sobre los derechos y normas aplicables al turista

Specifications

Size:
150mm x 215mm, 42 pages

Colour:
1-colour (black)

Paper:
three different coloured paper stocks, all recycled

Finishing:
screw binding

Binding:

SCREW BINDING

Congreso
de la Unión
de Abogados
Europeos
(UAE)
Programa
Hoteles
Inscripción
Eficacia y efectividad
de las normas aplicables
al derecho del turista

Palma de Mallorca

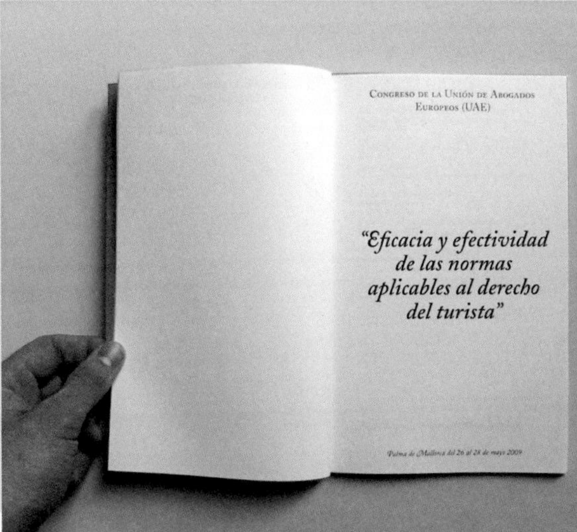
Congreso de la Unión de Abogados
Europeos (UAE)
"Eficacia y efectividad
de las normas
aplicables al derecho
del turista"
Palma de Mallorca del 26 al 28 de mayo 2009

Palma de Mallorca del 26 al 28 de mayo 2009

Design | **Client**

MIND DESIGN | PLAYLAB, UK

Title
Playlab Identity and Stationery

Specifications
Colour:
4 spot colours
Paper:
recycled paper stock
Finishing:
blind embossing, rubber stamped details

Format:

BLIND EMBOSSING

Paul Pethick
Unit 214
The Old Gramophone Works
326 Kensal Road
London W10 5BZ
T: +44 (0)7766 362 575
E: info@playlab.tv
W: www.playlab.tv
Activity 1: Dot-to-Dot
PLAYLAB

Title
Awards Annual

Specifications
Size:
250mm x 250mm, 500 pages
Colour & Print:
CMYK
Binding:
case bound, sewn sections
Finishing:
cover: drill holes and 4 foils

The cover idea came from the branding — a creative circle is a square. Because the book is an awards annual, the cover design took the form of a target. The various levels of awards are represented by foils — gold, silver, bronze and white for in-book. To further dramatise the target idea, holes have been drilled into the cover board.

Binding:

CASE BINDING

PRACTICAL GUIDE:

DESIGN & THE ENVIRONMENT

As demonstrated throughout this book, being environmentally conscious as a designer can be rewarding on many levels. Here are a few pointers of what to consider at various stages in the creative process.

Design:

Perhaps the most valuable part of the process is planning. There are a number of things you can do to reduce waste and costs during the design process by making conscious decisions on the following: the size of your item, the weight of the paper used, its planned life cycle (could it be easier to update, for example), and possibilities for multi-purpose uses. Equally important to the creative process is proofing the design thoroughly for any mistakes, therefore avoiding reprints and, of course, disappointments.

Print:

Being on good terms with your printer is vital, and the more you understand of the printing process the more creative you can be with your solutions. It is a good idea to get a printer involved with a project from early on. Using a local printer will help with reduced transport costs and emissions. Before sending the work to the printers, make a mock-up of the item in the studio. Seeing the design printed often shows mistakes that would be easy to miss onscreen.

Perhaps you have more than one project ready to print at the same time, maximising the use of inks, paper and energy. Even better, plan to make this the case. Print with vegetable-based inks if possible and make a considered choice when choosing metallic inks and foil blocking, as these may make the finished product impossible to recycle. Check your printer's green credentials for FSC certification and ISO14001.

Studio environment:
Design studios are like homes, not only in a sense of the time spent there but also in terms of the environmental choices we can make. There are green choices available for all aspects, including lighting, furniture, cleaning, heating and use of energy in general.

On top of the materials that we recycle at home, like milk cartons and newspapers, in a studio we can also find schemes to recycle CDs, DVDs (better still to eliminate these altogether and transfer files online), ink cartridges, computers, and all the paper (that you've used and used again and on both sides already, naturally).

From how we commute to work each day to what online hosting services we have chosen to use, all aspects can become part of a studio's environmental design ethos.

PRACTICAL GUIDE:

GLOSSARY

4/1:
One side of the sheet is printed in 4-colour and the other side is printed in 1-colour. Images and text are distributed according to the placement of 4-colour and 1-colour pages. This means the printing is more economical, as the book appears to be in colour, but half of it is in black and white.

4/1: p 70

4-COLOUR-PROCESS:
The process of combining four process colours – cyan, magenta, yellow and black – to create a printed full-colour picture or to create colours composed from these four colours. See also: CMYK.

BLEED:
A printed image or colour that extends past the trimmed edges of the page.

BLIND EMBOSS:
Blind embossing uses no foil when pressing the paper, creating a raised impression.

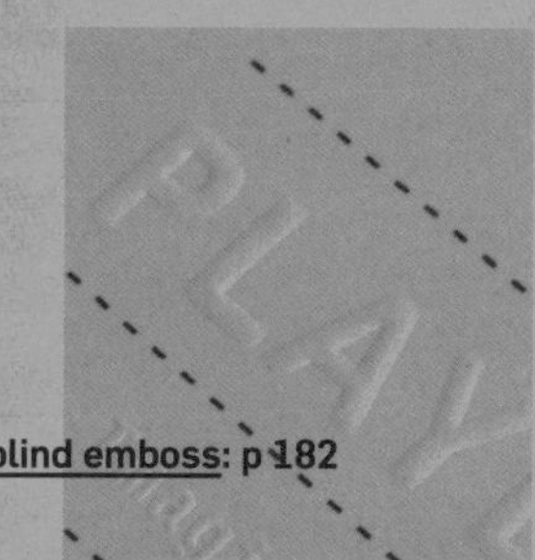
blind emboss: p 182

CASE BINDING:
The traditional binding process of making hard cover books, in which the book case (cover) is made separately from the text block and later attached to it.

case binding: p 184

CMYK:
CMYK (cyan, magenta, yellow, black) are the subtractive primaries, or process colours, used in printing. The printing process itself can also be described as CMYK.

DIE CUT:
Specially made shapes are cut into a paper or card using a steel die.

die cut: p 149

DIGITAL PRINTING:
Digital printing doesn't require printing plates, which means less waste and chemicals. Every digital print can be different, making it the economical choice for smaller print runs and one-offs.

DUOTONE:
Duotone image uses two colours only.

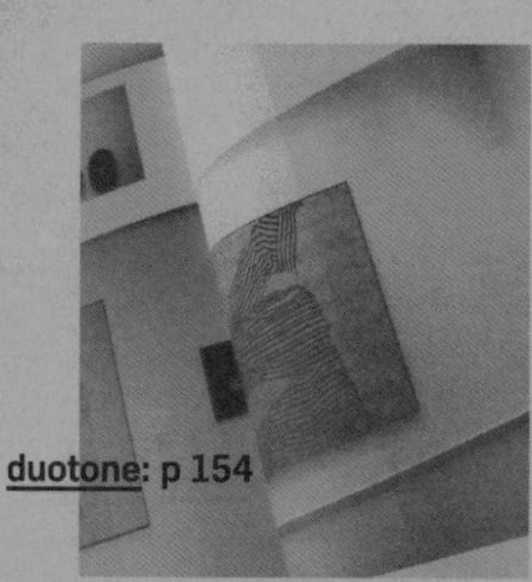
duotone: p 154

DUST JACKET:
Dust jacket is a loose outer paper wrap. It has folded flaps that hold it to the front and back book covers. Also known as a book jacket, dust wrapper or dust cover.

EMBOSS:
Embossing creates a raised image by pressing a shape into a sheet of paper with a metal or plastic die.

ENDPAPER:
Endpapers are the papers that attach a book block to the covers. These are glued onto the front and back inside covers.

FORE-EDGE:
Fore-edge is the part of a book opposite and parallel to the spine.

FULL BLEED:
A page that has an image that prints all the way to edges on all four sides. See also: Bleed.

dust jacket: p 142

full bleed: p 134

FOIL BLOCKING:
A technique to apply an image or text to paper or board using foil and a heat die.

FSC:
FSC (Forest Stewardship Council) is an independent, non-governmental, not-for-profit organisation established to promote the responsible management of the world's forests. FSC has developed principles for forest management of forest holdings, and a system of tracing, verifying and labelling timber and wood products, which originate from FSC certified forests.
www.fsc.org

FSC CHAIN OF CUSTODY:
FSC Chain of Custody (CoC) tracks FSC certified material through the production process – from the forest to the consumer, including all successive stages of processing, transformation, manufacturing and distribution. The FSC label provides the link between responsible production and consumption and thereby enables the consumer to make socially and environmentally responsible purchasing decisions.
www.fsc.org

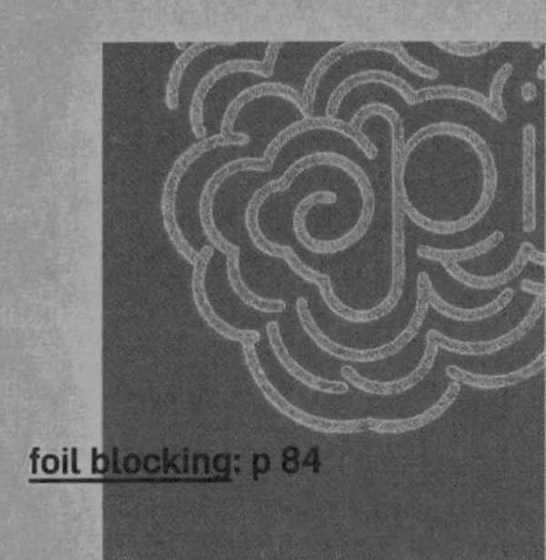
foil blocking: p 84

FRENCH FOLD:
The method of folding a sheet of paper in half and binding along the open edges. A french fold brochure is made by folding a page in half in one direction and then folding the folded page in half again in the opposite dimension.

HALFTONE:
A process used to reproduce an image through the use of dots varying either in size or in spacing, to simulate tonal range.

HEADBANDS AND TAILBANDS:
A functional and/or ornamental cloth tapes at the top and bottom of a book, between the spine and book block.

ISO 14001:
The ISO 14001 is a family of internationally-recognized standards for environmental management systems that is applicable to any business or organisation, regardless of size, location or income. These standards are developed by the International Organization for Standardization (ISO).
www.iso.org

french fold: p 104

headbands: p 128

LASER CUTTING:
A precise method of cutting that uses a laser to cut materials. Laser cutting allows elaborate and tiny shapes to be cut out of paper.

LETTERPRESS:
A traditional method of printing type, using a surface with raised letters (metal or wood) which is inked and pressed into the paper. The type debosses the paper in the process.

LOOP STITCH:
An alternate saddle-stitch binding method in which the staples are formed into wire loops, allowing a saddle-stitched publication to be bound in a standard 3-ring binder. They can also be customplaced for any 2-hole or 3-hole ring system.

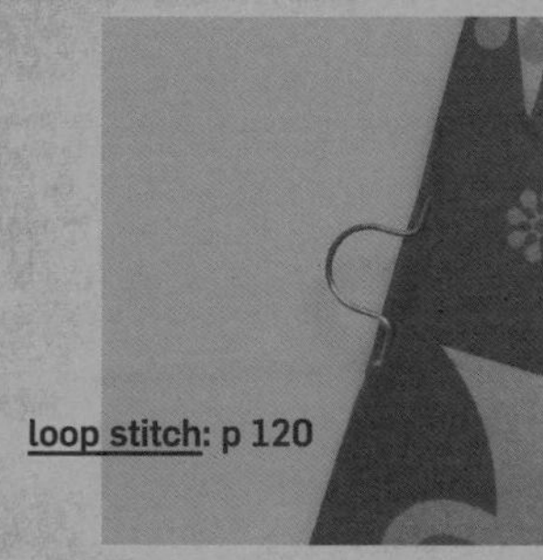
loop stitch: p 120

OFFSET:
Offset printing is a commonly used printing technique where the inked image is transferred (or "offset") from a plate to a rubber blanket, then to the printing surface.

PAPERLUX™ PAPER ETCHING:
Paperlux™ patented paper etching with bundling light creates pin-sharp, three-dimensional engravings on finest paper without hurting it's reverse side. The method removes defined parts of the upper layer in different depths and creates delicate relief in an unknown precision. This environmentally friendly techinique uses no colours, solvents or other materials, just light.

PEFC:
PEFC (Programme for the Endorsement of Forest Certification Schemes) is an international, not-for-profit organisation that is primarily made up of representatives of the forest products industry. Unlike the FSC, it does not set specific standards but is an umbrella brand that incorporates different national forest certification schemes. This is intended to make the forest certification easier and more applicable to different types of forests.
www.pefc.org

paperlux™ paper etching: p 178

PERFECT BIND:
A type of binding that glues the edge of individual sheets on the spine with glue.

PERFORATED PAPER:
Paper with regularly punched holes. It is also sometimes referred to as punched paper.

PMS:
PMS (Pantone Matching System) is is the most well known system of spot colours. It provides designers with swatches for specifying the match colours and gives printers the recipes for making them.

POST-CONSUMER WASTE:
Post-consumer waste is the recovered, recycled material a consumer has used and disposed of. There are recycled paper grades that range from 10% post-consumer to 100% post-consumer recycled.

perfect bind: p 112

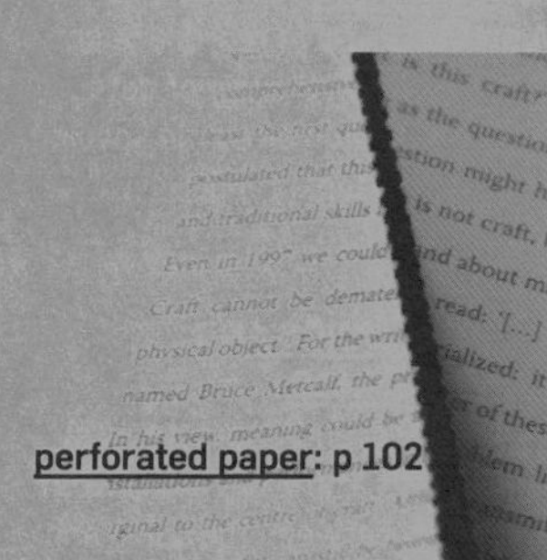
perforated paper: p 102

PRE-CONSUMER WASTE:
Pre-consumer waste is generated during the paper-making process, it's material that never reached the consumer. This waste can be from the mill or paper waste from the printers, such as off-cuts, that is returned to the mill for use as a pulp substitute. There are recycled paper grades that range from 10% pre-consumer to 100% pre-consumer recycled.

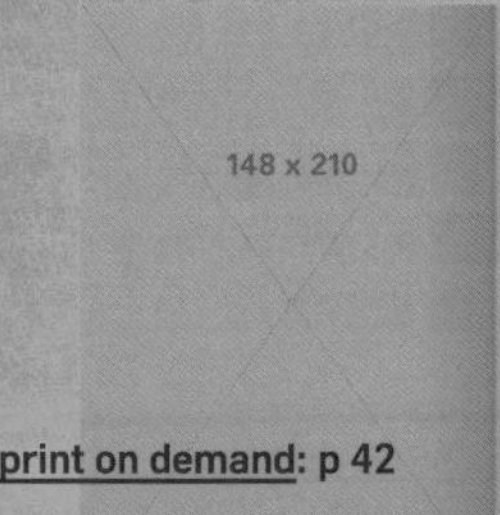

print on demand: p 42

PRINT ON DEMAND:
Digital print on demand is used as a way of printing items when required, for a fixed cost per copy, irrespective of the size of the order (which can be as low as one).

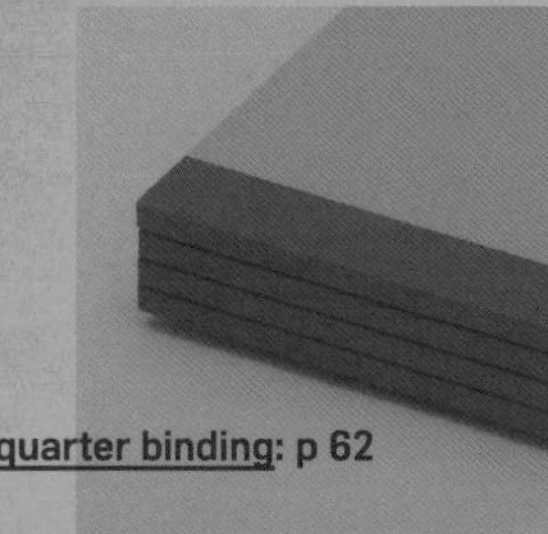
quarter binding: p 62

QUARTER BIND:
A book with its spine bound in a different material than the boards, so that the material on the spine wraps approximately one-quarter of the way around the front and back cover.

REAM:
500 sheets of paper.

RECYCLED PAPER:
Recycled paper is a broad term with multiple variations. In simplified terms, recycled paper is a grade of paper that contains recycled (post-consumer and/or pre-consumer) fibre, defined by percentages.

recycled paper: p 60

RGB:
RGB stands for the three primary colours of light – red, green and blue. The computer's native colour space for capturing images and displaying is refered to as RGB.

rubber stamp: p 166

RUBBER STAMP:
A stamp, usually made of rubber, that is inked and used for imprinting a design on another object by hand.

SADDLE STITCH:
A common method of binding where the cover and pages are bound together using stitches or wire staples on the centerfold.

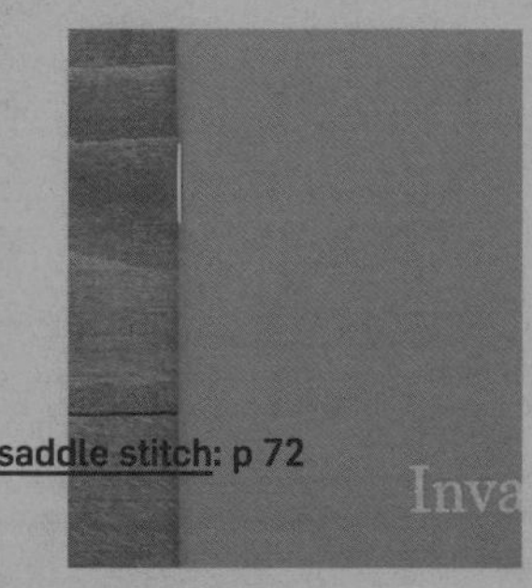
saddle stitch: p 72

SCORE:
A creased line in a sheet of paper that will allow folding at a specific point. It also helps to prevent cracking on the folds.

SEWN SECTION:
Also known as "thread-sewn section". A book in which each signature is sewn and then collated with other signatures and sewn together before binding.
See also: Signature.

SHEET-FED PRESS:
A printing press that prints individual sheets of paper as opposed to rolls.

SCREW BINDING:
A method of binding where the pages are kept together using bolts inserted through drilled holes and secured on the reverse side.

SIGNATURE:
A sheet with several pages printed on it; it folds to page size and is bound with other signatures to form a book.

sewn section: p 52

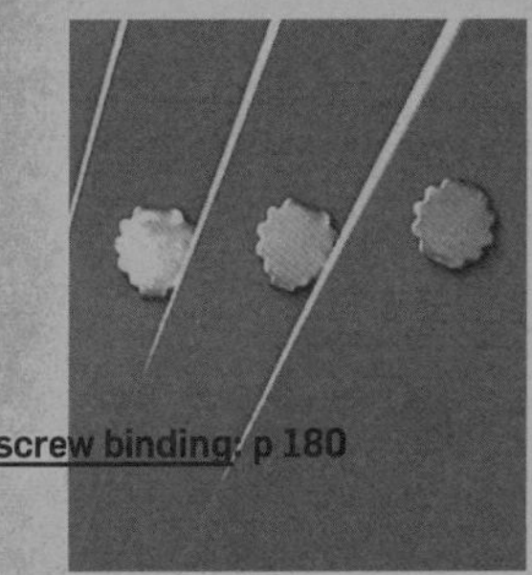

screw binding: p 180

SILKSCREEN:
Otherwise known as screenprinting, silkscreen is a printing method where ink is passed through a screen containing an image and onto a substrate.

SINGER SEWN:
The binding of a book using an industrial sewing machine, sewing along the binding edge.

SINGER SEWN THROUGH:
The binding of a book using an industrial sewing machine, sewing through the front of a book to the back.

SOY-BASED INKS:
Inks derived from soy bean oil instead of petroleum products, thus being easier on the environment. One of many vegetable-based inks.

SPINE:
The bound edge of a book.

silkscreen: p 57

singer sewn through: p 152

SPOT COLOUR:
Any specific ink not generated by the 4-colour process method. The Pantone Matching System (PMS) is the most well known system of spot colours used in graphic design.

SPOT UV VARNISH:
UV varnish applied to chosen areas of a printed piece.

SWISS BINDING:
With Swiss binding, the cover is not attached to the face top edge, completely detached and the binding edge has an attractive cloth lining enclosing the sheets together. This is another form of perfect binding.

THREE-HOLE SEWN:
A handmade binding method where binding thread is sewn into the spine through three holes and is fastened with a knot on the inside.

THREAD-SEWN:
See: Sewn Section.

three hole sewn: p 69

UV VARNISH:
UV (ultra violet) varnish is applied after printing, either as an overall finish to give a high-gloss finish, or applied as a 'spot' varnish to certain previously printed images.

VEGETABLE-BASED INKS:
Inks derived from vegetable oils instead of petroleum products, thus being easier on the environment.

VIRGIN FIBRE:
Fibre produced for the first time from wood.

WEB PRESS:
A printing press that prints on rolls of paper passed through the press in one continuous piece rather than individual sheets.

CONTACTS:

STUDIO INDEX

Hudson-Powell
London, United Kingdom
www.hudson-powell.com
page: 90

Isabel van der Velden
The Hague, the Netherlands
www.i-am-isa.nl
page: 86

Joe Stephenson
Nottingham, United Kingdom
www.joestephenson.co.uk
page: 56

Jorge Lorenzo Diseño y Comunicación Visual
Soto de Llanera, Spain
www.jorgelorenzo.net
page: 154

Julia
London, United Kingdom
www.julia.uk.com
pages: 92, 104, 110, 172

Kenn Munk
London, United Kingdom
www.kennmunk.com
page: 125

La Fabrica de Diseño
Madrid, Spain
www.lafabricadigital.com
page: 30

Lucienne Roberts +
London, United Kingdom
pages: 50, 54, 64, 140

Luke Elliott
Nottingham, United Kingdom
www.thisisluke.co.uk
page: 56

Marko Jovanovac
Opatija, Croatia
www.markojovanovac.com
page: 160

Mind Design
London, United Kingdom
www.minddesign.co.uk
page: 182

Monique Kneepkens
Brisbane, Australia
www.monswork.com
page: 134

müeller,weiland
Düsseldorf, Germany
www.muellerweiland.de
page: 58

Nivard Thoes
Hong Kong
www.nivardthoes.com
page: 166

Optimastudio
Madrid, Spain
www.optimastudio.com
page: 128

Patric Sandri
Zürich, Switzerland
www.patricsandri.com
page: 66

Pau Lamuà
La Bisbal d'Empordà, Spain
www.paulamua.com
page: 162

Pentagram
London, United Kingdom
www.pentagram.com
page: 118

re-public
Copenhagen, Denmark
The book is produced in collaboration with Romeo Vidner at re-public (design), noCUBE (publisher) Kristinehamns Konstmuseum, Ystad Konstmuseum, Nordin Gallery, Svensson, Ystad Centraltryckeri, Kristinehamns Konstmuseums Vänförening, Ystad Konstförening, Svenska Kyrkan and Norrstrands Stift.
www.re-public.com
page: 100

Sarah Boris
London, United Kingdom
www.sarahboris.com
page: 108

Sommese Design
Port Matilda, Pennsylvania, USA
page: 55

Studio Baer
London, United Kingdom
www.studiobaer.com
pages: 106, 112

Studio EMMI
London, United Kingdom
www.emmi.co.uk
pages: 36, 120, 136, 146, 149

Tangent Graphic
Glasgow, United Kingdom
www.tangentgraphic.co.uk
page: 144

The Luxury of Protest
London, United Kingdom
www.theluxuryofprotest.com
page: 28

This is Real Art
London, United Kingdom
www.thisisrealart.com
pages: 170, 184

THIS IS Studio
London, United Kingdom
www.thisisstudio.co.uk
pages: 60, 62, 98

Toby Edwards
Nottingham, United Kingdom
www.tobyedwards.co.uk
page: 56

unfolded
Zürich, Switzerland
http://unfolded.ch
pages: 27, 32, 72, 156, 158

Via Grafik
Wiesbaden, Germany
www.vgrfk.com
page: 153

vijf890 ontwerpers
Schiedam, the Netherlands
www.vijf890.nl
page: 102

Visual Think
Salt Lake City, Utah, USA
In partnership with the University of Utah graphic design students
www.carolsogard.blogspot.com
page: 48

Webb & Webb
London, United Kingdom
www.webbandwebb.co.uk
page: 122

Wire
London, United Kingdom
www.wiredesign.com
pages: 115, 132, 138

Worldstudio
New York, USA
www.worldstudioinc.com
page: 152

NOTES:

ACKNOWLEDGMENTS

THANK YOU:
Many thanks to all the designers who submitted work for inclusion in *Common Interest: Documents*.

Credits are due to **Jere Salonen** who took the folding format photos for the Introduction chapter, and to Studio EMMI's editorial consultant, **Henrietta Thompson**.

Thank you for the whole team at Index Book.

SPECIAL THANKS:
I want to thank Elsa, Jere, Äiti and Isi for the lifelong support.

This book is for Ramon Marin. Thank you for all you are.